College Kids Cook

Carol Field Dahlstrom

Carol Field Dahlstrom
Brave Ink Press
Ankeny, Iowa

College Kids Cook

Carol Field Dahlstrom

Author and Editor
Carol Field Dahlstrom

Book Design
Lyne Neymeyer

Photography: Andy Lyons Cameraworks, Dean Tanner—Primary Image
Contributing Writers: Elizabeth Dahlstrom, Carol McGarvey
Graphic Illustrations: Allison May, Lyne Neymeyer
Copy Editing/Consulting: Nancy Degner, Janet Figg, Jennifer Peterson
Proofreading: Kelli Chesnik, Michael Dahlstrom, Jill Philby
Recipe Development and Testing: Elizabeth Dahlstrom, Ardith Field, Barbara Hoover
Props and Location: Roger Dahlstrom
Technical Assistant: Judy Bailey

ISBN 0-9679764-5-6
Library of Congress Control Number: 2005900454

Separation: Scan Graphics, Des Moines, Iowa, U.S.A.
Printed in Singapore
First Edition

While all of the recipes and information have been checked and tested, human error
can occur. Carol Field Dahlstrom Inc. and Brave Ink Press cannot be held responsible
for any loss or injury associated with the making of recipes or other information
in this book.

Carol Field Dahlstrom, Inc. and Brave Ink Press strive to provide high quality products
and information that will make your life happier and more fulfilling. Please write
or e-mail us with your comments, questions, and suggestions or to inquire about
purchasing books, at braveink@aol.com or Brave Ink Press, P.O. Box 663, Ankeny, IA 50021.

Visit us at www.braveink.com to see upcoming books and information from
Brave Ink Press or to purchase any of our books.

Brave Ink Press—the **"I can do that"** books

You Can Cook!

Congratulations. You are holding a recipe book in your hands that you can really use. If you have never cooked before (but you like to eat), this is for you. If you are a pretty good cook (and you like to eat), this is still for you. If you hate to cook but are tired of carry-out pizza, this book is for you. These recipes have all been developed and tested by college kids just like you—well maybe not exactly like you. But college kids have tried these recipes and have given their ideas on how to make them work better for real College Kids.

College is a time in your life that you have very little time, very little money, and are usually hungry. You probably haven't had to cook much before. It's time to start cooking for yourself. These recipes are good, easy, and cheap. We have tried them out on all kinds of college kids—big football player types, arty non-conformist types, desperate I-just-want-a-date types, genius computer-nerd types, thin vegetarian-eater types, nervous I-don't-have-time-to-eat types, super student I-want-to-keep-my-brain-cells types, and frantic I-hope-I-don't-flunk-out types. They all liked the food!

We know you'll have fun making the recipes in this book and you might learn somthing along the way. So grab a bowl, a spoon, some ingredients and invite some friends over to prove that College Kids Cook!

Carol Field Dahlstrom

About this Book
Before you start cooking, there are a few explanations and assumptions that you should know. So please, read this.

Microwaves vs. Stoves
In this book you'll find recipes that you can really make. We know that most of you have a microwave and some of you have a full kitchen with a stove and oven. We hope you all have a refrigerator—hopefully with a freezer compartment. Some of the recipes can be made in either a microwave or a conventional stove/oven while others require one or the other. Whatever the case, there are plenty of yummy recipes for you to make no matter what cooking equipment you have.

Salt and Pepper
Sometimes we tell you to use salt and pepper and sometimes we don't. If a recipe absolutely must have it—and will taste terrible without it—then we put it in the list. Sometimes when the recipe calls for canned soups or sauces, we think there is plenty of salt already in the recipe. Add more if you want to. It is all a matter of taste—and because you have such good taste, we let you decide. We suggest that you add a little first (like a pinch). You can always add more, but it isn't easy to take the salt or pepper back out of the finished food.

Microwave-safe Bowls
When we tell you to use a small or large bowl, we are assuming it is microwave-safe. It doesn't have to be if it is just for mixing, but if you are only going to have a few bowls in your kitchen, make them microwave-safe. That way you don't have to worry about it. We are assuming that you know not to put any metal (including foil) in the microwave. Many old dishes (that Grandma or Mom gave you) may not be microwave safe either. And not all plastics are okay. Some will melt, especially if you are warming up food with a lot of fat in it.

Use Potholders
You know what a potholder is. If not, see page 14. Anyway, use them anytime you use the oven and even when you use the microwave. Depending on what kind of bowl you are using in the microwave and how long it is in there, it can get hot! Even when you are just cooking on top of the stove, have a potholder handy. The handles of pans can get hot, too. Sometimes we remind you of that in the instructions, but not always. We know you know it.

Turn Off the Stove and Oven When You are Done!

Of course, you know to do this. Sometimes we remind you in the recipe, and sometimes we don't. We usually mention it when there are many parts to the recipe and you might be thinking of something else. When you are done cooking, before you leave for class, go to bed, or just sit down to study, double check and see that you have shut off the stove, oven, or any other appliance. It's okay to check twice.

Checklists

With each recipe you'll find a checklist. We have given you the best possible information for how long it takes to make the recipe, how long you can wait before you do the dishes, what to do with leftovers, and how much it costs to make the recipe. These things will vary a bit. Of course it depends on how fast you move and how hungry you are, how dirty you can stand your kitchen, what type of refrigerator and freezer you are using, where you shop, or if your Mom and Dad give you a lot of food. Use the checklist as a guide.

Be Safe

In the back of the book we talk about food safety. But remember that safety when you cook is also about not setting the house on fire or getting burned or leaving the gas on after you are done using the gas stove. You must be thinking and alert when you are cooking. Be safe around all cooking items. Fires can start easily if you put a pan with oil in it on the stove and then answer the phone, or if your oven malfunctions, or if you are so tired from studying for finals that you forget to turn off the coffee pot. Always have a fire extinguisher handy. No, not in the closet. Put it under the sink or by the stove. Always have a big box of baking soda near the stove. Baking soda or salt will put out a small fire almost immediately. If a fire or other situation gets out of control, dial 911. That is what it is there for. Okay, now get cooking.

Find it

It's About the Basics   10-17

You don't need a lot of supplies, but you do need a pan or two—and a spoon is good, also. Here you'll find the necessities and the niceties of what stuff you need in your kitchen or dorm room before you start to really cook.

1

Poor and Hungry Out of Money   18-41

If all you have is chump change, you can still fill up on good food. From Peanut Butter and Banana Pancakes to Tomato Basil Soup, these recipes all cost very little but fill up the starving college kid.

2

5 Ingredients (or Less)   42-67

All of the recipes in this chapter use five ingredients or less! (Count them!) Quick Stir Fry, Simple Mac n' Cheese, Tuna Casserole, Pizza Boats, and Good Ol' Chili are just a few of these easy-to-make recipes.

3

Late Again! Take it With You   68-85

Even if you overslept again, you can latch on to some good food to take with you for the day. The make-ahead Power Bars, Hot Cocoa Mix, or even the Loaded Veggie Sandwich will make your day go much better.

Whether you think of yourself as an awesome cook or have trouble boiling water, this book is filled with great recipes that everyone will want to make—'cause they taste great and don't cost much money! They've all been tested by college kids just like you. Enjoy!

Read the Box and Make it Better!  86-103

Start with a package mix or product and then add your own cooking talent to make Sugar and Spice Biscuits, Peanut Butter Brownies, Corny Corn Bread, and more.

Eat Your Fruits and Veggies (Mom said!) 104-123

Your mother would be proud to see you create that Fruit Pizza, those Awesome Baked Apples, a Veggie Quesadilla, or any of the other amazing (and good for you!) recipes in this chapter.

Impress Your Friends! Feeling Creative? 124-143

Filled with simple ideas to serve at parties as well as other times when you want to impress your fellow students, you'll find a Fancy Yogurt Parfait, Chocolate-Covered Crispy Ball, Chocolate Chunk Cookies, and more.

Stuff You Need to Know (Just Read it!) 144-173

You know a lot, but this chapter tells you all about food safety, tips on cooking meat, pasta, and veggies, how to clean up really well—you'll even find a helpful chart or two.

Make It This Size 174-177
Glossary 178-181
Mom's Recipes 182-185

101 Answers 186-187
Index 188-191

It's About the Basics

You have to know the rules before you can play. Yup, and you have to know some very basic things before cooking makes sense. In this chapter you'll find some show-and-tell about the basic equipment you should have on hand in your kitchen—some must-haves and some just-nice-to-haves. You'll also find a list of foods to have in the cupboard that will make your cooking experience a little easier. So forge ahead, you can't go back now. You're ready to cook.

Basic Cooking Equipment

Before you start cooking you really need to have some basic equipment on hand. On pages 14–15 you will see the Elements of Basic Cooking Equipment. Memorize it. Make flash cards if you must. Well, maybe that isn't necessary, but you do need to have some basic stuff on hand if you really want to get cooking. On the next page you will see some lists. The first list is all you really need. But the other things are fun to have. So ask Mom or Dad if they have some extra items you can have—it just makes it easier and more fun.

Things You Really Need to Have

- baking pan
- can opener
- foil
- fork
- frying pan
- measuring cups
- measuring spoons
- microwave-safe bowl
- paper towels
- plastic bags
- potholder
- saucepan
- scrubber
- sharp knife
- spatula
- spoons
- storage containers
- table knife

Nice to Have

- blender
- cookie sheet
- corkscrew
- cupcake/muffin cup liners
- custard cups
- cutting board
- dish cloth
- dish towels
- disposable pans
- grater
- hand mixer
- ice cream scoop
- liquid measuring cups
- muffin/cupcake tin
- plastic wrap
- rubber scraper
- strainer
- timer
- toaster
- waxed paper
- whisk

Kind of a Luxury but Really Fun to Have

- canisters
- kitchen scissors
- lemon squeezer
- lots of bowls and pans
- rolling pin
- sandwich griller
- slow cooker such as a Crock Pot

Ask Grandma for these:
- a set of spices
- big brightly colored mixer
- food processor
- ice cream freezer
- ice crusher
- lots of money
- matching set of dishes
- matching silverware
- new kitchen towels
- panini maker
- place mats

The Elements of Basic Cooking Equipment

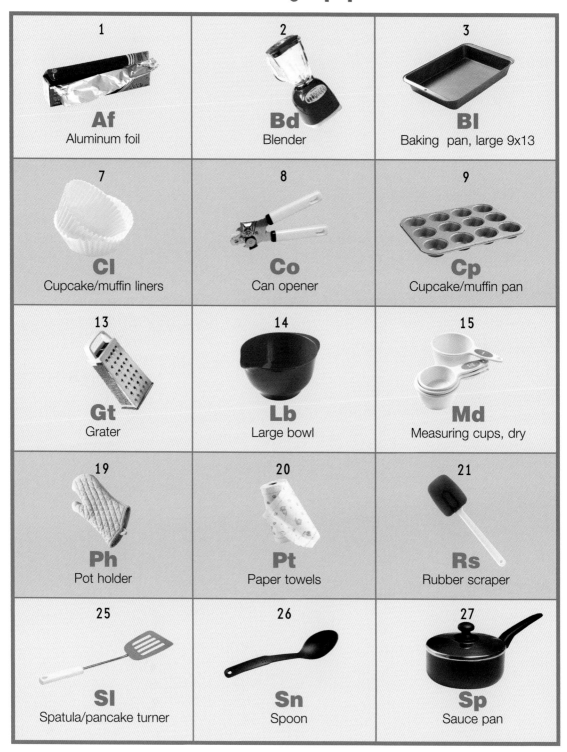

1	2	3
Af Aluminum foil	**Bd** Blender	**Bl** Baking pan, large 9x13

7	8	9
Cl Cupcake/muffin liners	**Co** Can opener	**Cp** Cupcake/muffin pan

13	14	15
Gt Grater	**Lb** Large bowl	**Md** Measuring cups, dry

19	20	21
Ph Pot holder	**Pt** Paper towels	**Rs** Rubber scraper

25	26	27
Sl Spatula/pancake turner	**Sn** Spoon	**Sp** Sauce pan

(things you really need and a few more!)

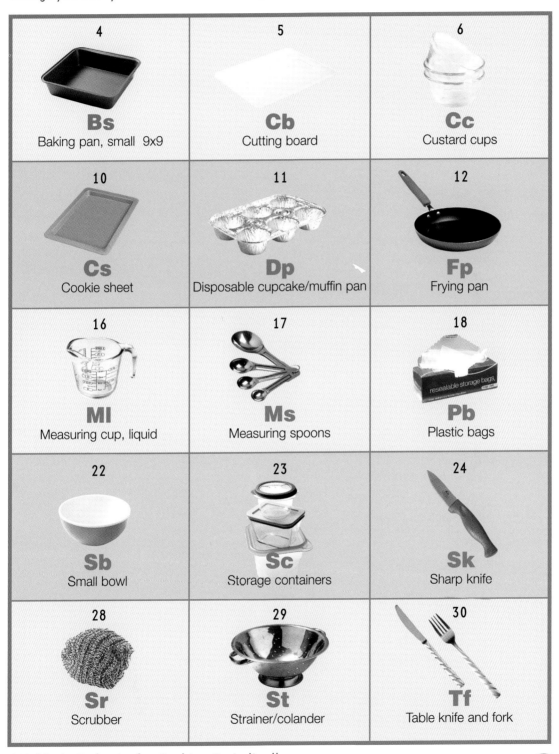

4	5	6
Bs	**Cb**	**Cc**
Baking pan, small 9x9	Cutting board	Custard cups
10	11	12
Cs	**Dp**	**Fp**
Cookie sheet	Disposable cupcake/muffin pan	Frying pan
16	17	18
Ml	**Ms**	**Pb**
Measuring cup, liquid	Measuring spoons	Plastic bags
22	23	24
Sb	**Sc**	**Sk**
Small bowl	Storage containers	Sharp knife
28	29	30
Sr	**St**	**Tf**
Scrubber	Strainer/colander	Table knife and fork

A Table to Refer to for Cooking Periodically

Basic Supplies (Food) to Have on Hand

When you are in the mood to cook, you want the ingredients at your fingertips. Of course you can go to the store every time you want to cook, and you will need to go for fresh items. But if you are going to get into this cooking thing, have some basic food on hand.

In the Cupboard or on the Shelf	In the Fridge	In the Freezer
Baking Items: • baking powder • baking soda • brownie mix • brown sugar • cake mix • cooking oil • flour • powdered sugar • salt • spices • sugar (granulated)	• butter • cheeses • eggs • fresh fruit • fresh veggies • ketchup • lettuce • mayonaise • milk • mustard • orange juice • pickles • salad dressings • sauces such as picante or salsa	• bagels • bag of frozen fruit • boneless chicken breasts • flour or corn tortillas • frozen veggies • ground beef • hot dogs • ice cream • loaf of bread

Other Stuff that is Good to Have on Hand

Pasta, Breads, and Crackers:
- buns or bread
- egg noodles
- lasagna noodles
- macaroni
- Ramen noodles
- soda crackers
- spaghetti

Canned Items:
- canned chicken
- Canned fruits
- canned soups
- canned tuna
- canned vegetables
- spaghetti sauce

Jars of Stuff:
- jelly
- peanut butter
- pickles

Other Stuff:
- coffee
- cold cereals
- microwave popcorn
- oatmeal
- pepper
- rice (both regular and instant)
- tea bags
- and, of course, candy

Poor and Hungry

Okay, so money is a little tight right now. But that doesn't mean you have to quit eating. There are all kinds of good recipes that use ingredients that cost very little—and they taste great, too. So break an egg, pour a pancake, slice a hot dog, or stir up some rice— food never tasted so good! Who knows, maybe you'll have money left over to pay back your roommate!

Peanut Butter and Banana Pancakes Checklist

 Time: About 15 minutes if you have the ingredients in your kitchen.

 Washing Dishes: Wash your sticky plate and silverware right away. After the griddle or frying pan has cooled, just wipe it clean with a damp cloth.

 Leftovers: The leftover batter will keep in the fridge for about 3 days. Put the leftover cooked pancakes between layers of waxed paper and put in a plastic bag in the freezer. They will keep for up to a month. To reheat, place one or two pancakes at a time in the microwave for about 20 seconds or less. If you heat too long they will get rubbery.

 Cost: The pancake mix, peanut butter, and bananas cost about $1.25 for the amount needed for about 10 pancakes, or about 12 cents a pancake. Real maple syrup is expensive, but the flavored kind is just pennies a serving.

Peanut Butter and Banana Pancakes

If you skip your 8:00 class, you may have time to make these. Otherwise, make them for dinner or for a Saturday morning treat.

Kitchen stuff you need:

Frying pan or griddle

Pancake turner

Food you need:

No-stick cooking spray
such as Pam
1 container Bisquick
Shake n' Pour
Pancake Mix
Peanut butter
Ripe bananas
Maple syrup

Now do something:

1 Make the Shake n' Pour pancake mix by adding the water as directed on the package.

2 Spray the frying pan with cooking spray. Heat the pan over medium-high heat for about 60 seconds. The frying pan needs to be very hot. It is ready when a drop of water sizzles on it.

3 Pour about 1/4 cup of the pancake mix into the pan. It will spread out into a circle quickly. (Look on page 175 to see how big to make it.) Let the pancake cook for about 30 seconds. You will know to flip it over when the surface of the pancake has bubbles forming on it.

4 Flip the pancake over and let the other side cook about 30 seconds. Take it out of the pan and put it on a plate. Make as many pancakes as you want to eat. (Turn off the stove when you are done!)

5 Now take a pancake and cover it with peanut butter. Cut bananas in 1-inch slices and put on top of the peanut butter. Continue layering until you feel like stopping. Add some syrup and eat.

Chicken-Veggie Soup

Who says you can't make homemade soup? Well, kind of homemade. It may not be as good as Mom's but it still hits the spot!

Kitchen stuff you need:

Saucepan	Spoon

Can opener

Food you need:

- 1 10.75-oz. can condensed chicken vegetable soup
- 1 10.5-oz. can chicken broth
- 1 can water
- 1 package Ramen noodles (discard seasoning packet)

Fish crackers (optional)

Now do something:

1 In a large saucepan, combine the soup, broth, and water. Heat over medium-high heat until the soup is boiling, stirring occasionally. Boil 1 minute.

2 Now add the uncooked Ramen noodles and turn down the heat to medium-low. Heat and stir until the noodles are tender, about 2 minutes.

3 Turn the heat off and pour into bowls.

4 Add some fish crackers, if you wish. Makes 4 servings.

Chicken-Veggie Soup Checklist

 Time: About 10 minutes if you have the ingredients in your kitchen.

 Washing Dishes: These dishes wash up easily—so get at it!

 Leftovers: Cover and put the leftover soup in the refrigerator right away. It can keep for up to 3 days in the refrigerator. To reheat it, just put it in a microwave-safe bowl and heat it until hot.

Cost: The entire batch of soup costs about $1.60 without the crackers. That is 40 cents for each serving. The fish crackers cost about $2.00 for a sack, but even a few will make the soup look cute! You decide if it's worth another 25 cents per serving.

Other uses for Ramen noodles

- Cook the noodles in boiling water until tender (discard seasoning packet). Drain. Use with stir fry. (See Stir Fry recipe, page 48.)
- Cook the noodles in boiling water until tender (discard seasoning packet). Drain. Add ½ cup cooked frozen mixed vegetables, 1 tablespoon butter, ½ cup shredded cheese, and salt and pepper. Enjoy!

Quick Egg Sandwich

Make your own fast food—and it only costs about 30 cents! Eat up!

Kitchen stuff you need:

Small plate

Small bowl

Fork

Measuring spoons

Food you need:

1 tablespoon butter
1 large egg
1 tablespoon milk
Salt and pepper
2 tablespoons shredded cheese or 1 slice cheese
Two slices toast

Now do something:

1 Grease the small microwave-safe plate (about 6 or 7 inches in diameter) with the butter by spreading it with your clean fingers or a small piece of waxed paper.

2 Break the egg into the small bowl. Add the milk, salt, and pepper, and beat together with a fork until it is mixed really well.

3 Pour the egg onto the plate. Carefully put it in the microwave and cook on high for 1 minute. Take it out and flip the egg over. (It won't be quite done.)

4 Put the cheese on top and put it back in the microwave for 20 more seconds.

5 Put the egg between the two pieces of toast to finish your egg sandwich. Cut in half crosswise to make it look fancy.

Quick Egg Sandwich Checklist

 Time: This is so quick to make. Start your toast at the same time you start the egg. The egg sandwich will only take about 10 minutes to make—and you can eat it on your way to class!

 Washing Dishes: There are only the plate and the utensils—nothing to complain about here.

 Leftovers: There won't be any.

 Cost: Would you believe an egg only costs about 9 cents? That is a lot of protein for the money! The cheese is about 10 cents. The two pieces of bread are about 10 cents. So with a little bit of butter and milk, you have a 30-cent meal. Amazing!

Eggs 101
(answers on page 186)

1. **Which came first, the chicken or the egg?**
   A. Chicken B. Egg

2. **Eggs have the highest quality protein of any food.**
   A. True B. False

3. **What are those beautifully decorated eggs called?**
   A. Fabulous B. Forbidden C. Fabergé

4. **Where was Eggs Benedict first served?**
   A. Perkins B. Alice's Restaurant C. Delmonico's

Stuffed Potato

A potato can be your friend—and you'll both be stuffed.

Kitchen stuff you need:

Knife   Scrubber

Food you need:
Large baking potato
What you like to put in the potato such as:
Butter
Cottage cheese
Sour cream
Shredded cheese
Broccoli
Tomatoes
Mushrooms
Peppers
Seasonings such as salt, pepper, onion salt
Leftovers such as chili, veggies, and chopped meats work well recycled on top of the potato.

Now do something:

1 Any potato will work for a baked potato but certain varieties are better than others. Big potatoes are the best value. As you science- and math-types know, there will be more volume per surface area. For you music and art majors, that means more to eat!

2 Wash the potato well. Don't use soap, but do put it in the sink and rub it with a clean scrubber and warm water. If there are rotten spots, cut them out. The potato won't be perfectly smooth when you are done washing—it should just be clean.

3 Use the knife to make several slits in the potato so it doesn't explode in the oven or microwave. *To cook in the microwave,* put the potato right on the microwave tray (or on a paper towel if you are feeling tidy). Depending on the size of the potato—and it makes quite a difference, use these times for

the microwave: 12 minutes for a large potato, 8 minutes for a medium, and 5 minutes for a small. You know it is done when a fork slides easily into the potato.

To cook in the oven, just put the potato right on the rack and bake it for about 1 hour at 350 degrees. You will know it is done when a fork goes in easily.

After the potato is done, cut a slit in the top and open it up. Fill it with the butter and cheese first, then the rest of the goodies. Eat right away.

Stuffed Potato Checklist

Time: If you use the microwave, about 15 minutes should do it. The oven takes about an hour.

Washing Dishes: There are no dishes. Yes!

Leftovers: There probably won't be any, but if you really want to keep what is left, put it in the refrigerator immediately and warm it up in the microwave later in the day or the next day. Throw it away after that. Potatoes spoil quickly. Never leave a baked potato to cool on the counter. Always refrigerate immediately.

Cost: The potato only costs about 30 cents. The stuff you put on it can be very inexpensive or quite costly. For example, a bit of cottage cheese and a little butter doesn't cost much but cheese and tomatoes out of season may.

Tuna Melt Checklist

 Time: The time it takes from opening the can to sinking your teeth into this tasty treat shouldn't be more than 15 minutes.

 Washing Dishes: You just have to wash the bowl and spoon. No problem.

 Leftovers: Don't keep the leftover sandwiches if they are made—they'll get soggy. But you can refrigerate the tuna mixture in a closed container and keep it refrigerated for about 2 days. Use the mixture to make the sandwiches just like you did the first time.

 Cost: Depending on the quality of the tuna you buy, the cost for four open-faced sandwiches is about $1.40. That's about 35 cents per sandwich. Not bad. You can also use bagels or hamburger buns instead of English muffins, and these might even be a little cheaper.

Tuna Melt

What is it about tuna? It's cheap, comes in a can, and tastes really good. Can't ask for much more than that.

Kitchen stuff you need:

Can opener	Small bowl
Spoon	Knife
Paper towel	Measuring spoons

Food you need:

English muffins
Small can or bag tuna
3 tablespoons
mayonnaise
1 tablespoon sweet
pickle relish
2 slices American
cheese

Now do something:

1 Open the can of tuna. Drain the extra tuna liquid in the sink or the trash. If you put it in the sink, immediately run lots of hot water in the sink.

2 Put the tuna, mayo, and pickle relish in the bowl. Add some salt and pepper. Stir it together.

3 Open up the English muffin and lay it on the paper towel. Spread the tuna mixture on each piece of the muffin. Make it as full as you like. (You should be able to get four open-faced sandwiches from this recipe, but if you like, put it all on two!)

4 Lay a slice of cheese on top of the tuna mixture.

5 Put it in the microwave on the paper towel for about 20 seconds or just until the cheese melts. Makes 4 open-faced sandwiches.

Tomato Basil Soup

Wow, this sounds fancy and tastes great! You don't have to tell anyone how easy and cheap it is to make.

Kitchen stuff you need:

 Sharp knife | Saucepan

 Can opener | Spoon

Measuring spoons

Food you need:

2 tablespoons butter
1 tablespoon dried onion or
  2 tablespoons chopped fresh onion
1 tablespoon dried or freeze-dried basil or
  2 tablespoons chopped fresh basil
1 tablespoon flour
2 14.5-oz. cans petite diced tomatoes
1 14-oz. can chicken broth

Oyster crackers (optional)

Now do something:

1 If you are using fresh chopped onion and/or basil, set it aside. (Look on page 157 if you don't know how to cut up veggies—there are some good tips!)

2 Put the butter in the saucepan. Okay, you're going to learn to sauté. It sounds hard but it isn't. Put the saucepan on the stove on medium-high until the butter melts.

3 Immediately put in the onion and basil. Stir until the onion and basil start to brown. There, you did it. (You obviously didn't need help, but if you want to, look on page 158 for tips on how to sauté veggies.)

4 Now, immediately add the flour and stir it in only until it is blended. Take the pan off of the heat and take a deep breath. This is real cooking!

5 Slowly add the chicken broth while you stir the mixture. Put the pan back on the stove and turn to high heat. Stir constantly until the mixture boils. Boil 1 minute.

6 Now add both cans of tomatoes. Bring back to a boil and then reduce the heat immediately to let the soup simmer (that means gently boiling—see page 181 for a real definition) for about 5 minutes. Pour into bowls and eat right away! Makes 5 servings.

★ Note: To make this in the microwave, mix all of the ingredients together in a large microwave-safe bowl, leaving out the flour. Cook in the microwave until it boils—about 5 minutes. Stir occasionally to keep it from boiling over. It won't have the rich buttery sauté taste, and it will be a little thinner in consistency, but it will still taste good.

Tomato Basil Soup Checklist

 Time: If you make this soup on the stove, you will be doing a few more steps than if you are cooking in the microwave. Either way, you should be able to be eating soup in 30 minutes or less.

 Washing Dishes: Easy dishes to do—just one pan or bowl.

 Leftovers: Keep leftover soup in the fridge for up to 4 days. Reheat in the microwave.

 Cost: The whole batch costs about $3.00, so each serving is about 60 cents without the crackers. What a deal!

French Toast

Even if you are a Russian major, you can still eat this.

Kitchen stuff you need:

Large Bowl	Fork
Frying pan	Pancake turner

Measuring spoons	Measuring cups

Food you need:

2 eggs
2 teaspoons flour
1 teaspoon sugar
1 cup milk
Two slices of bread
2 tablespoons margarine

Now do something:

1 Crack the eggs into a cup or dish and then put them in the big bowl. (See page 154 on how to crack an egg.) Beat with a fork. Add the flour and sugar to the egg mixture and beat until they are well blended. Add the milk. It will seem like there isn't much in the bowl, but you'll need the space when you dip the bread—you'll see.

2 Put the bread (both slices) in the bowl of egg mixture. (We used cinnamon raisin bread. You can use whatever kind of bread you like.) Be sure it is all in the egg mixture.

3 Put the margarine in the frying pan and put the pan on the stove on medium-high heat until the margarine melts. Be sure the bottom of the pan is covered with the margarine.

4 Lift the pieces of bread out of the egg mixture (they will be soaked with the mixture) and put them in the hot pan. You should hear a frying sound. Lay one piece beside the other if you have room in your pan. If not, fry one at a time.

5 As soon as one side of the bread is lightly browned (this only takes about 1 or 2 minutes), turn it over and brown the other side. Let that side brown and then take it out of the pan. You're ready to eat! (Don't forget to turn off the stove!) Makes 1 serving.

French Toast Checklist

Time: This is quick—about 15 minutes if you hurry.

Washing Dishes: Just the frying pan and bowl. Really easy to wash.

Leftovers: French toast doesn't keep very well in the fridge. You can freeze the cooked piece (wrapped in a plastic bag or waxed paper) in the freezer for up to a month and reheat it for a few seconds in the microwave if you want.

Cost: Two pieces of yummy homemade French toast is about 35 cents. Wow, can't beat that!

Things to put on your French Toast

- Powdered sugar
- Cinnamon
- Jelly
- Sugar
- Peanut butter
- Fresh fruit
- Honey
- Syrup
- Whipped cream
- Slice of ham
- Brown sugar

Rice Pudding

Yes, even you can make this comforting food and feel all warm and cozy inside.

Kitchen stuff you need:

 2 small bowls | Measuring spoons

 Measuring cups | Fork

 Spoon | Oven safe custard cups

Food you need:

1 cup water
1 cup instant rice such as Minute Rice
1 egg
1 cup milk
1/4 cup brown sugar
1 teaspoon cinnamon
1/4 cup raisins

Now do something:

1 Preheat the oven to 325 degrees. Put the water in the microwave-safe bowl and put it in the microwave until it boils—about 2 minutes depending if you started with hot or cold water. Take it out of the microwave and add the instant rice and stir together. Cover it with a lid or paper towel for about 5 minutes. This will allow the rice to soak up the water.

2 While you wait, break the egg into the other bowl and beat it with the fork. Add the milk and mix it together.

3 Add the brown sugar, cinnamon, and raisins to the milk mixture. When the rice is done, add it to the milk mixture. Stir it all up and put it in the custard cups. It should fill four cups.

4 Put the custard cups in the oven for about 20 minutes. You will know they are done when the pudding is set and there isn't any liquid left. (To be sure they are done, put the tip of a table knife in the center of the pudding. If it comes out clean, it is done.) Take out of the oven. Eat the pudding warm with milk or eat cold.

Note: If you don't have custard cups, put the pudding in a 8x8-inch baking pan. Bake in the oven for about 25 minutes. You'll know when it is done when it is set and there isn't any liquid left. (See page 161 to read about the magic table knife method of testing custard type puddings). Makes 4 servings.

Rice Pudding Checklist

Time: From the time you make the instant rice to the time you sit down to eat this creamy treat, about 45 minutes. Well worth the wait.

Washing Dishes: You only need to wash the fork and bowls now. The little custard cups are a bit harder to do, so let them soak after you eat the pudding. Then they will wash up easily.

Leftovers: Cover the pudding that is left and keep it in the refrigerator. You can eat it warm or cold. It won't keep very long—only about a day. The rice breaks down after that.

Cost: Rice and eggs are cheap. This entire pudding is about 35 cents. You can eat lots.

Rice 101
(answers on page 186)

Q. 1. Wild rice is the longest form of brown rice.
A. A. True   B. False

Q. 2. Throwing rice at weddings means what?
A. A. That the wedding was too long
B. A wish for prosperity and abundance
C. Good luck to the future kids

Q. 3. Rice is cholesterol-free.
A. A. True   B. False

Q. 4. When did people start eating rice?
A. A. 4000 BC B. 1776 C. 1955

Hot Dog Bagel

Combining a good old hot dog with cheese and a bagel is a no-brainer. Delicious!

Kitchen stuff you need:

Sharp knife | Paper towel

Food you need:
1 hot dog
1 plain bagel
1 slice Provolone
    cheese
Barbecue sauce

Now do something:

1 Open up the bagel and lay it on the paper towel. Use a sharp knife to cut a hole out of the center of the slice of cheese. Put the cheese ring on the bagel bottom.

2 Slice the hot dog into little pieces and arrange them on the cheese. (Yes, you can make a design, art majors.)

3 Put the top on the bagel sandwich and put it in the microwave for 30 seconds.

4 Take out the sandwich, open it up, and cover it with barbecue sauce. Makes 1 serving.

Hot Dog Bagel Checklist

 Time: From the time you unwrap the hot dogs until the time you are wiping the barbecue sauce off your jeans, it will be about 15 minutes.

 Washing Dishes: There are really no dishes to speak of—just wash the knife and put it away.

 Leftovers: There probably won't be any, but if you really want to keep what is left, put it in the refrigerator immediately and warm it up in the microwave later in that day or the next.

 Cost: The sandwich costs about 30 cents. You can also make these on English muffins or on a hamburger bun.

Bagels 101
(answers on page 186)

 1. A bagel is the only bread that
A. has a hole in the middle.
B. is chewy. C. is boiled before it is baked.

2. When bagels were first invented in Poland, who were they to be served to?
A. Pregnant women B. Prisoners C. Beggars

3. A bagel contains almost no
A. carbohydrates. B. fat. C. protein.

Microwave Oatmeal

Make this in the same bowl that you eat it in—no dishes and a yummy treat!

Kitchen stuff you need:

Small bowl | Spoon

Measuring spoons | Measuring cups

Food you need:
½ cup oatmeal (rolled oats)
(old-fashioned or quick)
⅔ cup milk
1 teaspoon brown sugar

Stuff to put in your oatmeal: jelly, chocolate chips, raisins, nuts of any kind, honey, or fresh fruit (optional)

1

Now do something:

Measure the oatmeal and put it into a microwave-safe bowl large enough so it won't boil over when cooking. You can spoon out the oatmeal into another bowl to eat out of when it is done, or you can just mix everything in the bowl that you will be eating out of. Make sense?

2

Add the milk and brown sugar. Mix it all up well.

3

Put it in the microwave for about 2 minutes or until it bubbles. Stir it once while it is cooking.

4

Remove from microwave (it will be hot—use a potholder), and add whatever goodies you like!
Makes 1 serving. How easy is that?

Microwave Oatmeal Checklist

 Time: This is a quick dish to make. From measuring to eating is about 8 minutes. (You'll even have time to brush your teeth before you go!)

 Washing Dishes: You only have the one you mixed it in and the one you ate out of. If that bowl was the same, you only have that and the spoon!

 Leftovers: You can refrigerate what is left and warm it up later that day or the next, but it does get a little gummy. It is probably better to just throw away what you don't eat.

Cost: Would you believe 15 cents? If you add raisins, jelly, or anything else, it will cost a little more.

Oatmeal 101

(answers on page 186)

 1. **What is the ultimate comfort food?**
A. Oatmeal   B. Oatmeal   C. Oatmeal

 2. **Is the man on the Quaker Oats box William Penn?**
A. Yes   B. No   C. It is his twin

 3. **What year was instant oatmeal introduced?**
A. 1926   B. 1946   C. 1966

 4. **What's the top non-cereal use for oatmeal?**
A. Meat loaf   B. Cakes and pies   C. Cookies

Ways to Save Some Bucks

Buying the food and other stuff you need is kind of like a game. Think of ways you can save money and still get most of the things you need. You'll feel like a winner!

- Don't go to the grocery store on an empty stomach—you'll buy a lot of things you don't need. Everything looks absolutely delicious when you are really hungry.

- Set a budget before going to the supermarket. Bring a calculator to keep tabs, if that works for you. At least bring a list of what you need to buy and about how much you can spend. If you get to the check-out lane and you don't have enough money, just tell them and they will return some of the items back to the shelf for you. It happens all the time.

- Endcaps, or ends of the aisles, often display something new or something in season. Don't be tempted if it's not something you want or need.

- Stay focused on your purchases by making a list and sticking to it. Don't buy the prettiest packaged food or something you saw advertised on television if you don't need it. (Unless, of course, you had a bad week and you need a treat!)

- Take eggs and milk from the back of the case. Older merchandise tends to be pushed forward. Check expiration dates carefully on dairy products and eggs. You don't want to waste money by having to throw it out!

- If you can afford to buy in bulk (that means to buy lots of one item at a time) the unit cost will usually be less. Think about shopping with a friend so you can take advantage of buying this way.

- If you use coupons, remember—it's not a bargain if you didn't need it or weren't going to buy it in the first place. Many times coupons are a way for you to try a product, not to save money.

- Shop seasonal items, particularly in the produce aisle according to where you live. Strawberries and seedless grapes are inexpensive in the summer in the Midwest, for example, but costly in winter.

- Buy non-grocery items like facial tissues, shampoo, and toilet paper at discount stores. Grocery stores usually charge a bit more.

5 ingredients

It doesn't take a lot of stuff to make good food—just the right stuff. There are certain simple combinations that just taste great together. So have a few basics on hand and with the awesome recipes in this chapter you can create a decent—even delicious—meal.

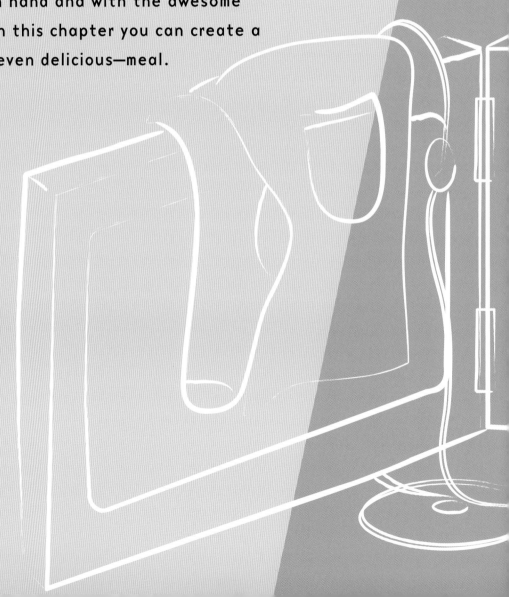

Just Good Spaghetti

You'll be making this a lot. Getting everything cooked at the same time is the trick.

Kitchen stuff you need:

Frying pan | Saucepan

Spoon | Strainer

Food you need:

1 pound ground beef
1 26-oz. jar spaghetti
sauce
1 package spaghetti
(use what you want)
Shredded Parmesan
cheese

1

Now do something:

Fill the large saucepan half full with hot tap water. Add a dash of salt. Put it on the stove and turn the burner to high. While you are waiting for the water to boil, put the ground beef into the frying pan. Add a little salt and pepper. Put the frying pan on the stove. Cook the meat on medium-high heat until it is cooked thoroughly—you shouldn't see any pink left in the meat. Keep stirring the meat as it cooks. (See page 153 for hints about cooking meat.) After it is completely cooked, drain off any fat or liquid carefully into the garbage—not in the sink. It may clog it up.

2

Put the meat back on the stove and add the jar of sauce. Cook until it bubbles. Cover it and turn down the heat to low while you cook the pasta. Stir it once in a while.

3

The water should be boiling by now. (If it is boiling before you are done making the sauce, turn down the heat.) How much pasta you cook depends not only on how hungry you are, but also on the size of your saucepan. (Look on page 151 for tips on

cooking pasta.) Bring the water to a full boil (if it isn't by now) and add the pasta. Turn down the heat to medium. Watch it carefully, stirring it to keep it from boiling over. It will take about 6 minutes before it is done. You can test it by carefully lifting out a piece of pasta with a fork and cutting it in half. It should be limp but not gummy. Don't overcook—it gets mushy. When it is done, carefully pour off the hot water into the sink or pour the spaghetti into a strainer.

To serve, put the spaghetti on the plate, spoon the meat sauce over the pasta, and sprinkle with cheese. Makes about 6 servings.

Just Good Spaghetti Checklist

 Time: This will take about 30 minutes to get everything done just right.

 Washing Dishes: They are all easy to do—nothing is sticky.

 Leftovers: You can mix the leftover pasta and sauce together and then divide it into individual servings to eat later. Cover and keep in the refrigerator for about 3 days. Or you can freeze it and reheat it later, too. It will keep in the freezer for up to 6 months.

 Cost: Depending on the sauce you buy, each serving costs about 50 cents.

Real Simple Mac n' Cheese

Yes, the stuff from the box is pretty good, but once you make this homemade kind, you'll never go back!

Kitchen stuff you need:

Small Bowl

Measuring cups

Measuring spoons

Knife

Spoon

Food you need:

½ cup elbow macaroni
⅔ cup warm water
3 1-inch cubes of processed cheese such as Velveeta
2 tablespoons milk
Salt and pepper

1 **Now do something:**

Place the macaroni and warm water in the microwave-safe bowl. Cook in the microwave on high for 3½ minutes. The water will boil and bubble up, so be sure and choose a bowl that has high enough sides or is large enough so it doesn't bubble over.

2 Take the macaroni out of the microwave. Add the cheese, milk, and salt and pepper. See the list at right for other things to add to your dish. Put it back in the microwave for about 1 minute more or until the cheese is melted.

3 Take the finished macaroni and cheese out of the microwave and stir until cheese is completely melted. Makes 1 serving.

Real Simple Mac n' Cheese Checklist

 Time: This is really quick to make. You can be eating the macaroni and cheese in about 8 minutes.

 Washing Dishes: You can actually eat out of the same bowl as you cook the mac and cheese in. Yup, you can. So the dishes are very few.

 Leftovers: Since you're only making one serving, there probably won't be any, but if there is, it will keep covered in the fridge for about 2 days.

 Cost: This is pretty cheap. The macaroni costs about 8 cents. The cheese is the expensive part, but it still only costs about 20 cents. The milk is pennies. So one cheesy bowl of this good stuff is about 30 cents. If you add peas or whatever, it will be just a little more.

Other Stuff You Can Put in Your Mac n' Cheese

- 1/4 cup frozen peas
- 1/4 cup cubed ham
- 1/4 cup frozen veggies
- Slices of hot dog
- Cut-up pieces of cooked chicken
- Diced tomatoes

Quick Stir-Fry

Stir this up on top of the stove for a quick, hot, filler-up meal.

Kitchen stuff you need:

Sharp knife | Plastic bag

Small bowl | Frying pan

Measuring spoons | Fork

Food you need:

**2 boneless chicken
    breast halves
2 tablespoons flour
2 tablespoons oil
1 can green beans
1 bag frozen vegetables**

**Cooked Ramen noodles
(optional)**

Now do something:

1 Rinse the chicken breasts and cut them into about 1-inch pieces with the knife. (See page 174 for about what size to cut them.) It doesn't matter if the pieces are exactly the same but they will cook more evenly if they are all about the same thickness. After you are done cutting up the chicken, be sure you clean up the work area and wash your hands and utensils with soap and hot water.

2 Put the flour in the plastic bag. Add a dash of salt and pepper or other <u>seasonings</u> if you like.

3 Drop the chicken into the bag of flour and shake the bag to cover the pieces with the flour. Set the bag of chicken aside.

4 Get the veggies ready: Open the can of beans and drain the liquid off. Put about 1/2 cup of beans into a small bowl. Add about 1 cup of the frozen veggies. Mix them together. (Put the remaining frozen veggies back in the freezer and extra beans in the fridge to cook later.) Set the bowl of veggies aside.

Place the oil in the pan and turn the heat on the stove to medium-high. Drop the chicken into the oil in the pan. Cook the chicken until it is done, turning it with the fork to keep it from burning. This will only take about 4 or 5 minutes. When the fork easily goes into the chicken and you see no pink meat, you know it is done.

Pour the veggies from the bowl into the frying pan. Keep stirring the mixture until the vegetables are hot and cooked. This will take about 3 more minutes. Put over cooked Ramen noodles or eat by itself. Whatever you do, eat it right away. Makes 2 servings.

Quick Stir-Fry Checklist

 Time: If you have everything you need on hand, this only takes about 20 minutes to make.

 Washing Dishes: Just throw the plastic bag away—so all you have to wash is the frying pan and bowl. Get at it!

 Leftovers: This really doesn't keep too well. If you don't mind soggy noodles and vegetables, you can keep it covered in the fridge and eat it within a day or two.

 Cost: A chicken breast costs about 50 cents and you only use a portion of the frozen veggies. Green beans are about 60 cents a can, and you'll have some left over here, too. Total cost for one serving—about 80 cents.

Hot Spiced Applesauce

Add a little spice to an already favorite dish. You're going to love it!

Kitchen stuff you need:

Small bowl

Measuring spoons

Spoon

Measuring cups

Food you need:

1 cup plain applesauce
1 tablespoon sugar
1/2 teaspoon cinnamon
Handful of raisins

1

Now do something:

Note: Applesauce comes in all sizes of jars and even in little individual containers. The most inexpensive way to buy it is in a large jar. Because you probably can't eat all of it before it spoils, buy a medium-sized jar. Don't buy the individual serving size for this recipe—it costs too much.

2

Measure the applesauce into the bowl. Put the rest back in the refrigerator.

3

Add the sugar, cinnamon, and raisins and stir it up well.

4

Put it in the microwave for 1 minute until it is warm. Makes 2 small or 1 large serving—go ahead, eat it all now.

Hot Spiced Applesauce Checklist

Time: This is so easy. Even if you have to go to the store to buy the applesauce first, you'll still be eating in no time. If you have all of the ingredients, this takes about 8 minutes to make.

Washing Dishes: You'll probably eat out of the same bowl you heated the mixture in, so just a bowl, measuring spoons, and a spoon.

Leftovers: Refrigerate anything left over. It will keep for about 3 or 4 days. Just reheat in the microwave for a few seconds to warm it up.

Cost: For both servings, about 25 cents.

2 5 Ingredients

Hot Spiced Applesauce

(answers on page 186)

1. **Applesauce goes best with**
A. Pork. B. Beef. C. Vegetarian dishes.

2. **Applesauce dates back to**
A. the Civil War. B. the Vietnam War C. Medieval times.

3. **According to the Bible, what spice did Moses use?**
A. Nutmeg B. Cinnamon C. Paprika

4. **What culture was willing to pay a lot for cinnamon?**
A. Egyptians B. Greeks C. Romans

Pizza Boats

Yes, they look like boats—well kind of, and they are super-easy to make and fill you up fast.

Kitchen stuff you need:

Frying pan

Cookie sheet

Aluminum foil

Pancake turner

Spoon

Food you need:
1 pound ground beef
1 can pizza sauce
2 hoagie-style buns
1 small bag shredded cheddar cheese

Now do something:

1 Turn the oven on to 425 degrees. If you don't have an oven follow the microwave instructions after step 5.

2 Before you start to cook the meat and sauce, get the hoagie buns ready. Cover the cookie sheet with foil. Open the hoagie buns cut side up and lay them on the foil. If they need to be sliced, slice them the long way (so they look like a boat—that's how they got the name). You can fit all 4 half buns on the cookie sheet.

3 Put the ground beef into the frying pan. Add a little salt and pepper. Put the pan on the stove. Cook it on medium-high heat until it is cooked thoroughly—you shouldn't see any pink left in the meat. You need to keep stirring the meat as it cooks. After it is completely cooked, drain any fat off the meat. Drain it carefully into the garbage—not in the sink. (See page 153 for hints for cooking meat.)

4 Add the can of pizza sauce to the meat. Stir it up and heat the mixture on the stove just until it bubbles. Take it off the stove and spread a little of the mixture on each part of the hoagie bun. Sprinkle each sandwich with about 2 or 3 tablespoons of cheese.

5 Put the pan in the oven for about 10 minutes or until the cheese starts to bubble. Use a potholder and take the cookie sheet out of the oven. Makes 4 big open-faced sandwiches.

Note: If you don't have an oven, you can put one sandwich at a time in the microwave on a paper towel for 1 minute or until the cheese is melted. Yum.

Pizza Boats Checklist

 Time: From start to finish, if you use the oven, it will take about 25 minutes before you are eating the sandwich.

 Washing Dishes: Because you were so smart to use the foil, just throw that away. The cookie sheet should be clean. If you used the microwave, you're home free.

 Leftovers: Wrap in plastic wrap and reheat in the microwave for about 20 seconds. They will keep in the fridge for about 2 days before they get a little soggy.

Cost: The cost for one sandwich is about 75 cents, depending on where you shop.

Chicken and Rice

This old-time fave just got easier. Use canned chicken and canned soup and all is well.

1 Now do something:

Turn on the stove to 350 degrees. Open the can of chicken and the can of soup. Pour them into the bowl.

2 Add the water and the uncooked rice and stir everything together. (See page 179 to learn about the difference between real and instant rice.) Add some pepper if you like. The condensed soup provides enough salt.

3 Pour it all in the baking pan. Cover the pan with foil.

4 Put the pan in the oven. After the first 20 minutes, take the foil off and stir. Put the foil back on, and put back in the oven for the last 20 minutes. (It will bake for a total of about 40 minutes.) You know it is done if it is bubbly and hot. Remove from oven (use potholders.) Don't forget to turn off the oven! Makes about 5 servings.

Note: If you want to be creative, try some toppings on your casserole such as onion rings from a can, cashews, sliced almonds, crushed potato chips, or shredded cheese. Just cook the casserole as directed above and when it is done, put the topping on the finished casserole. Put it back in the oven for 5 more minutes. Take out of the oven and eat.

Chicken and Rice Checklist

Time: From the time you open the can of chicken and the can of soup until you are lifting that first bite of yummy casserole—about 1 hour.

Washing Dishes: The baking pan may take a little work after the meal is over, but the bowls and spoons are easy to do. Put some water in the baking pan and let it soak a bit to make it easier to wash.

Leftovers: Place the leftover chicken and rice in a covered container in the fridge and it will keep for up to 3 days. Just reheat in the microwave. Only reheat the portion you will eat.

Cost: The entire casserole costs about $2.75 or about 55 cents per serving.

The Best Beanie Weenies

Yes, you read it here first—these are the best beanie weenies ever!

Kitchen stuff you need:

 Small bowl	Spoon
Sharp knife	Can opener

Measuring spoons

Food you need:

1 can pork and beans
2 tablespoons catsup
1 tablespoon mustard
**1 tablespoon brown
    sugar**
3 hot dogs

Now do something:

1 Open the can of pork and beans and pour them into the microwave-safe bowl (or pan if you are using the stove). If the beans seem to have a lot of liquid on them, pour a little out and throw it away.

2 Add the catsup, mustard, and brown sugar to the beans and mix it all up well.

3 Cut up the hot dogs into bite-size pieces and mix them into the bean mixture.

4 Put the bowl into the microwave for about 5 minutes or until it bubbles, or place the pan on the stove on medium-high heat until it bubbles. You're ready to eat!
Makes 3 large servings.

Time: From opening the can of beans to eating this tasty little treat is about 15 minutes.

 Washing Dishes: Whether you cook them in a bowl in the microwave or in a pan on the stove, these dishes are easy to wash.

 Leftovers: This classy dish will keep in the fridge for about 3 days. Just reheat in the microwave.

 Cost: Total cost for the entire batch is about $1.00 or around 34 cents per serving.

2 5 Ingredients

Hot Dogs 101

(answers on page 186)

Q.• 1. **How many hot dogs do Americans consume on July 4th?**
A. A. 50 million   B. 75 million
C. 150 million

Q.• 2. **What European town claims to be the origin of the hot dog?**
A. A. London   B. Paris   C. Frankfurt

Q.• 3. **What dog is called the wiener dog?**
A. A. Terrier   B. Dachshund
C. Springer spaniel

Pita Treats

Make a pita sandwich for yourself and sit back and relax. You've studied enough!

Kitchen stuff you need:

Small bowl	Spoon

Measuring cups	Sharp knife

Food you need:

1 cup shredded cheese
½ cup black olives
½ cup ham cut into little pieces
2 pita breads

Italian Dressing (optional)

Now do something:

1. Note: You can use any type of ham you like. Ham comes sliced in packages, at the deli, or in chunks. If you buy it in chunks, it is a lot cheaper. Whatever you buy, cut it into small pieces using a sharp knife. (Look on page 176 to see about how big to cut them.)

2. In the small bowl, mix the cheese, olives, and ham together.

3. Open up the pita bread and spoon the mixture into the opening of the bread.

4. Put the sandwich in the microwave and heat for about 30 seconds or until the cheese is melted.

5. Remove the sandwich and serve with a little Italian dressing if you want. Makes 2 pita treats.

Pita Treats Checklist

 Time: This is quick—about 10 minutes from start to finish. If you really want to make it quick for later in the week, have the ham cut up into small pieces and keep in a closed container.

 Washing Dishes: Just the bowl and spoon. Easy, huh?

 Leftovers: You can keep the extra cheese mixture refrigerated for a day or two. Make only the sandwiches that you need. The cheese will get soft and gooey if you keep the mixture any longer than that.

 Cost: About 50 cents per half sandwich.

Pitas 101
(answers on page 186)

 1. What shape is pita bread?
A. Round   B. Rectangular   C. Square

 2. Where did pita originate?
A. Grocery store   B. Middle East   C. Montana

 3. How does the "pocket" form inside?
This is an essay question.

 4. How versatile is pita bread?
A. Use as a spoon to dip hummus   B. Wrap gyros, falafel, turkey, or anything   C. Stuff tuna or chicken salad inside

The Perfect Burger

Every now and then you just need an All-American burger. You'll love this one.

Kitchen stuff you need:

Large bowl	Fork
Frying pan or grill	Spatula

Food you need:
1 pound ground beef
¹/₂ packet dry onion soup mix
Hamburger buns

1

Now do something:

Put the ground beef in the bowl. Add the **¹/₂** packet of dry onion soup mix. Mix together with a fork until it is blended well. If you use your hands to mix the meat, be sure to wash your hands very well before and after.

2

Make the ground beef into patties. (To see a good size for a hamburger pattie, see page 174.) To do this, place a ball of the meat mixture between two pieces of waxed paper and smash it down with your hands. Or you can just form the shape with your hands. (That is why they need to be clean!) One pound of hamburger makes four medium-sized burgers.

3

Always cook ground beef to be well done. The center of the hamburger is usually where the beef is undercooked. Here is a trick. After you make the beef pattie, put a hole in the center by poking it with your clean finger. This way, the heat will move through the burger more evenly. (See page 153 for tips on cooking meat.)

4 You can cook the burger on the grill or in a frying pan. To fry the burgers, turn the heat to medium-high and place the patties in the pan. Stand there and watch them as they cook, and when one side is brown, flip it over. Let that side brown and flip it again if necessary. Keep cooking until there is no sign of pink in the meat. To cook on the grill, cook in the same way, turning when one side is browned. Continue to turn until the meat is all browned.

5 Put the hamburgers on the buns. Serve with any kind of toppings you like such as cheese, catsup, mustard, onions, tomatoes, pickles, ranch dressing, thousand island dressing, or just plain mayonnaise. Delicious!

The Perfect Burger Checklist

 Time: It takes about 10 minutes to mix the burgers and 15 minutes to cook them—so you are eating the perfect burger in less than 30 minutes.

 Washing Dishes: Clean the frying pan right away after the meal. Wash the other dishes thoroughly as well. If you use the grill, remember it needs to be cleaned, too.

 Leftovers: Cold hamburgers keep in the fridge in a covered container for 3 or 4 days.

 Cost: Depending the quality and where you shop, ground beef is about $2.00 per pound. So with the spices and buns you'll have about 60 cents in each perfect burger.

Classic Tuna Casserole

These is just something about cheese and tuna all melted together that just can't be beat.

Kitchen stuff you need:

Can opener	Large bowl
Sharp knife	Saucepan
Spoon	Strainer

Measuring cups

Food you need:
Small can or bag tuna
1 10.75-oz. can
    condensed cream of
    chicken soup
1 can water
Five 1-inch cubes of
    processed cheese
    such as Velveeta
3 cups dry noodles

¹/₂ cup frozen peas
    (optional)

1 Now do something:
Open the can of tuna. Drain the extra tuna liquid in the the trash. Put the tuna in the microwave-safe bowl.

2 Add the soup, water, and cheese in the microwave safe bowl. (Look on page 174 to see how big to cut up the cheese.) Add some salt and pepper if you like and add the peas now if you are using them. Stir it all together until it is mixed up well. Set the tuna mixture aside while you cook the noodles.

3 Fill the saucepan half full of hot tap water. Put the water on the stove and turn the burner to high heat. It will take a minute or so before it starts to boil.

As soon as it begins to boil, add the dry noodles and turn down the heat to medium. Stand right by the stove and watch the pan carefully, stirring the noodles with the spoon to keep them from boiling over. They won't take long to cook—about 3 or 4 minutes. (Read the box or bag and follow what it says.) Don't overcook the noodles or they will become mushy. You know they are done when you can just bite through them. (For hints on cooking pasta see page 151.) Put the strainer in the sink. (Be sure the sink is clean!) Immediately remove the pan from the stove and pour the noodles into the strainer. Let them drain for a minute and then add the noodles to the tuna mixture. Stir it together.

Put the bowl in the microwave for about 8 minutes or until the cheese melts and the mixture starts to bubble. You will need to stir it a couple of times. Makes 4 servings.

Classic Tuna Casserole Checklist

 Time: You'll be eating in 25 minutes.

 Washing Dishes: Well, there are quite a few, but they aren't hard to wash.

 Leftovers: Leftover casserole will keep for a couple of days in the fridge. Just reheat in the microwave. Only reheat what you are going to eat.

 Cost: Depending on the quality of the tuna you buy, the cost for the entire casserole is about $1.95 or about 49 cents a serving.

Good Ol' Chili

When it is cold outside and you want something quick and hot, make some chili in just a few minutes and then get back to your studying. (Or play Nintendo.)

Kitchen stuff you need:

Frying pan	Saucepan

Can opener	Large spoon

Food you need:
- 1 28-oz. can diced tomatoes
- 1 24-oz. jar salsa
- 1 15-oz. can chili beans
- 1 pound lean ground beef

Shredded cheese, tortilla chips for topping (optional)

1 Now do something:

Open the cans and jars. Pour all of these ingredients into the saucepan. Set aside.

2 In the frying pan, cook the hamburger over medium-high heat, chopping and stirring it with a large spoon until all the meat is brown and you can see no pink meat. Add salt and pepper to taste. If the meat looks greasy, drain off the fat and liquid. Don't put the grease in the sink! Put it in an empty can or in the trash. (See page 153 for hints on cooking meat.)

3 Add the hamburger to the other ingredients in the saucepan. Stir it together and heat over medium-high heat until boiling. This will take about 5 minutes. Turn the heat down and simmer for another 5 minutes, stirring the mixture occasionally.

4 Remove the chili from the stove and put in bowls. Sprinkle some shredded cheese on top if you want and serve with tortilla chips. Makes 5 large servings.

Good Ol' Chili Checklist

Time: About 15 minutes if you have the ingredients in your kitchen.

Washing Dishes: At least put some water in the pans to soak. That will make the dishes easier to do tomorrow—but today is always good.

Leftovers: Some people think chili is better as a leftover because the flavors blend. Put the leftover chili in the refrigerator right away. (See food safety tips, page 146.) It can keep for up to 5 days in the refrigerator. To reheat it, just put it in a microwave safe bowl and heat it until hot.

Cost: Depending upon where you buy your groceries, the entire batch of chili costs about $5.00. That means (for you psych majors) that each serving is about $1.00. If you add cheese, add another 25 cents.

Chili 101

(answers on page 186)

Q. 1. **Where was chili first invented?**
A. A. San Antonio, Texas B. Iceland C. South America

Q. 2. **What popular northern ingredient in chili is absolutely forbidden in Texas?**
A. A. Salt   B. Beans   C. Buffalo

Q. 3. **When was chili first invented?**
A. A. 1820s   B. 1950s   C. Middle Ages

Q. 4. **Who first invented chili?**
A. A. Betty Crocker B. Edison C. Cowboys

Don't forget the salad. . .

When You Want to Cook!

When you feel like making a meal you want the ingredients there and ready to go! So have a few things on hand for when you get in the cooking mood!

- Canned Soups: Keep cream of celery, cream of chicken, cream of mushroom, and tomato soup on hand to eat or to use in casseroles. Many of these soups come in low-fat versions as well as the original versions. The low-fat type won't be as smooth and creamy as the original higher-fat content soup (but you will save some calories).

- Spaghetti Sauce: These handy sauces come in all kinds of flavors such as traditional, garlic, chunky, and on and on. They come in both plastic and glass jars or in cans. The canned version is by far the cheapest. Spaghetti sauce works great for lasagna sauce, quick spaghetti sauce (of course), and even for pizza sauce if you don't have the real thing in the cupboard.

- Pasta of all kinds: Pasta comes in dozens of shapes and sizes. It is cheap and is great to use in casseroles or just to cook and eat with butter or a sauce. Elbow macaroni, egg noodles, Ramen noodles, spaghetti, and lasagna noodles are just a few types of pasta to have on your shelf.

- Cheese: Cheese comes in every imaginable way and can be used in almost everything! It comes shredded, cubed, dried, in a block that is processed, or in a can. You can find Swiss, Cheddar, Parmesan, Provolone, Muenster, and literally dozens of other kinds. Most of these need to be kept in the refrigerator—so don't overbuy.

- Canned veggies and fruits: These are easy to have on the shelf, taste great, and can be used in so many dishes. Add a little cottage cheese and you almost have a meal!

- Frozen foods: Have a pound of ground beef, a few chicken breasts, and some hot dogs in the freezer and you can come up with a great meal anytime. A bag of frozen veggies comes in handy, too.

- Canned chicken and canned tuna: These keep on the shelf and are great for sandwiches and casseroles. Spend the extra money for high-quality tuna. You'll be glad you did!

Late Again! Take it With You

It doesn't matter if you are sitting in Psych class, walking to Chem lab, or meeting a friend at the library to compare notes, you get hungry everywhere. Rather than play the vending machine game, take your food with you. The recipes in this chapter can be made ahead of time and travel pretty well. So plan ahead a little—your stomach will thank you.

Take-Along Wraps

Make these ahead of time and have them ready to grab as you run out the door.

Kitchen stuff you need:

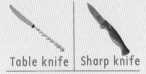

Table knife | Sharp knife

Aluminum foil or
plastic wrap

Food you need:

**Purchased flour tortillas
of any kind**

**Tub of cream cheese in
any flavor you like**

**All kinds of stuff you
like to fill the
wraps (see list on
opposite page)**

Now do something:

Wraps are easy and fun to make. Tortillas are inexpensive and come in many flavors. Choose the kind you like and fill them with a variety of things. To make the wrap, lay the tortilla flat and spread with a thin layer of cream cheese. Spread it to the edges. The cream cheese should be about $\frac{1}{8}$ inch thick.

Wash any fresh vegetables and chop them into small pieces. Drain any liquid from items that come in cans (such as olives) and chop them into small pieces. Put what is left back in the fridge.

Put whatever you wish on top of the cream cheese. Look at the list (opposite page) for ideas. If you are using ham or turkey, lay the slice on top of the cream cheese first, then add the other stuff. Don't fill the tortilla too full or it will be hard to roll up.

Roll up the tortilla. Lay it on a piece of plastic wrap or foil. Seal the foil or plastic and put it in the refrigerator until you are ready to eat it. When you are ready to eat it, unwrap and slice off what you want. Put it in a little plastic bag and go. If you use meat and are taking it with you, it will need to be carried in a cooler (unless it is winter and it is cold outside or you eat it within 2 hours).

Things to put in wraps: In one of our yellow (taco-flavored) tortillas we used chive cream cheese and yellow, red, orange, and green sweet peppers with green onions. In the other taco-flavored tortilla we used plain cream cheese with raisins, shredded carrots, and lettuce. In the plain flavored tortilla we used honey walnut cream cheese with turkey, dried cranberries, and lettuce. In the green (spinach-flavored) tortilla we used plain cream cheese, co-jack cheese, ham, and black olives. In the red (sun-dried tomato-flavored) tortilla we used plain cream cheese, red peppers, ham, broccoli, and mozzarella cheese.

Take-Along Wraps Checklist

 Time: These take only minutes to make if you have everything on hand and washed.

 Washing Dishes: This is awesome because you only have to wash the knife that spreads the cream cheese!

 Leftovers: Keep them in the refrigerator. These are basically designed to be leftovers because you can slice a piece off and leave the rest in the fridge. But after about 3 days they get soggy.

 Cost: The tortillas are really cheap, but what you put in them can add up. You only use part of the cream cheese, so one wrap costs about $1.00 if you use meat and more cheese.

Chewy Granola

Throw this chewy and yummy (and healthy!) snack in a bag and take it with you to munch on all day long.

Kitchen stuff you need:

Large bowl

Small bowl

Measuring spoons

Measuring cups

Spoon

Food you need:

2 cups old-fashioned oatmeal (rolled oats)
1 cup Crispix or Chex cereal, slightly crushed
²/₃ cup dried raisins
¹/₂ cup sunflower seeds
¹/₂ teaspoon cinnamon
¹/₄ teaspoon salt
¹/₄ cup apple juice
²/₃ cup brown sugar

Now do something:

1 In a large bowl, mix the oatmeal, crushed cereal, raisins, sunflower seeds, cinnamon, and salt. Set aside.

2 In a microwave-safe small bowl, mix the apple juice and brown sugar. Heat in the microwave for 1 minute or until just boiling. Stir the mixture very well to completely dissolve the sugar.

3 Pour the hot mixture over the oatmeal mixture. Mix it together well.

4 Put the mixture in the microwave for 1 minute. Remove and stir. Store in plastic bag in refrigerator or freezer. Makes about 4 cups.

Chewy Granola Checklist

 Time: Even though you have a lot of ingredients to assemble, you can still make this entire batch in about 20 minutes.

 Washing Dishes: There are just two bowls and a spoon, and all are easy to wash.

 Leftovers: Keep the granola in the fridge or freezer and just take out what you want when you want it. It will keep nicely for about 3 weeks in the fridge and about 6 months in the freezer. It may get a little chewier over time—but it will still taste good! It also makes a great breakfast cereal. Just add milk and enjoy!

Cost: The entire batch costs about $2.00 so each cupful is about 50 cents.

Other things to put in granola

- Dried cranberries
- Cashews
- Peanuts
- Rolled wheat
- Sesame seeds
- 1 teaspoon nutmeg
- Dried cherries
- Dried blueberries

Sweet Triple-Decker Peanut Butter Sandwiches

You know you love peanut butter—and even with a little candy added—it is still a good lunch!

Kitchen stuff you need:

Paper towel | Table knife

Sharp knife

Food you need:
3 slices of bread
Lettuce
Peanut butter
3 orange slice candies

1 Now do something:
Wash the lettuce and lay it on a paper towel to dry. Cut the candies into small sliced pieces.

2 Lay the three slices of bread in a row. Spread each slice with a thin layer of peanut butter.

3 On the left slice of bread, add the lettuce. On the right slice of bread, put the candies on top of the peanut butter.

4 Flip the left slice of bread on top of the middle slice of bread. Pick up those two and lay them on top of the right slice of bread with orange candies.

5 Put the sandwich in a plastic bag and take it with you for a great snack later in the day. Makes 1 serving.

Sweet Triple-Decker Peanut Butter Sandwiches Checklist

 Time: If this sandwich takes longer than 5 minutes to make, you're taking too long.

 Washing Dishes: Just the knives—no big deal.

 Leftovers: Only make what you can eat—these don't keep very well. However, if you must make it the night before, just add the lettuce in the morning.

 Cost: For one sweet triple decker sandwich—about 35 cents.

Other things to put on a peanut butter sandwich

- Jelly, of course
- Cinnamon-sugar
- Dried apricots
- Honey
- Thinly sliced apples
- Raisins
- Mayonnaise
- Shredded carrots

Hot Cocoa Mix

This makes a big batch of mix so take just a little with you and add hot water later in the day for a warm treat.

Kitchen stuff you need:

Large bowl | Spoon

Plastic bag | Measuring cups

Food you need:
- **3 cups non-fat dry milk**
- **2 cups sifted powdered sugar**
- **1 cup powdered non-dairy creamer**
- **1/2 cup unsweetened cocoa powder**
- **1 cup miniature marshmallows**

Now do something:

1 In a large bowl combine the non-fat dry milk, sugar, creamer, and cocoa powder. Stir together well. Add the marshmallows. The entire batch should make about 19 servings. Keep the big batch of mix in an airtight container or plastic bag.

2 To make just one serving, put 1/3 cup of the mixture in a resealable plastic bag. Put that bag in a paper cup or disposable cup to take with you.

3 To make the hot cocoa, empty the mix into the cup and add 1 cup very hot water. Stir until the powder dissolves. The marshmallows will float! You'll feel all cozy!

Hot Cocoa Mix Checklist

 Time: If you have everything you need on hand to make the whole batch, it will take about 15 minutes. To make one cup after the whole batch is made takes about 15 seconds!

 Washing Dishes: Easy to do—just rinse out the bowl. From then on you'll be making the hot cocoa in the cup you are drinking out of!

 Leftovers: This was made to be leftovers. Keep in an airtight contaner or bag.

Cost: For the whole batch, about $1.95 or about 10 cents a serving.

Chocolate 101

(answers on page 186)

 **1. Who was the first European to discover chocolate?**
 A. Christopher Columbus B. Marco Polo C. Tony Blair

2. In ancient Aztec times, cocoa beans were used as a medium of exchange. So if you had 4 cocoa beans, what could you buy?
A. A metal hatchet B. A gold nugget C. A turkey

3. Plain, unaltered chocolate tastes
A. sour.   B. bitter. C. sweet.

4. Which wise founding father raved about chocolate's "superiority...for both health and nourishment"?
A. Ben Franklin B. John Adams C. Thomas Jefferson

Loaded Veggie Sandwich Checklist

 Time: This is a masterpiece of a sandwich—but it will only take about 10 minutes. It may take some practice to keep it all from falling out. But don't worry, your artistic qualities will make it work, however.

 Washing Dishes: Just knives. Put them in the sink and do them tonight.

 Leftovers: You should only make what you can eat—these don't keep very well. You can make it the night before, however. It will keep fine overnight so you can grab it in the morning.

 Cost: For one healthy sandwich like this, about 50 cents if you buy the carrots shredded. If you do it yourself, even cheaper.

Carrots 101

(answers on page 187)

 1. **Where do carrots come from?**
A. Little bags in the store   B. The garden
C. Bunny Land

 2. **Who first made carrots orange?**
A. the Dutch   B. Moses   C. the French

 3. **If you eat too many carrots your skin can turn orange.**
A. True   B. False

 4. **Are baby carrots as nutritious as larger varieties?**
A. Yes   B. No   C. Only if they are grown in Wyoming

Loaded Veggie Sandwich

This sandwich has crunch and texture and it's good for you!

Kitchen stuff you need:

Paper towel | Table knife

Sharp knife

Food you need:

2 slices of whole wheat bread
2 tablespoons cream cheese
Shredded carrots
Sunflower seeds
Raisins

Now do something:

1 Lay the two slices of bread side by side on the paper towel. Use whatever bread you like, but whole wheat is probably the best.

2 Spread each slice with a thin layer of cream cheese—about 1 tablespoon per slice.

3 On the left slice, put on the shredded carrots. You can buy carrots already shredded, but if you want to shred them yourself, use a grater. (To see a picture of a grater, look on page 14.) Now sprinkle on the sunflower seeds and raisins.

4 Put the two slices of bread together and put in a sandwich bag. Cut in half if you like. You're set. Makes 1 sandwich.

Power Bar

This is a long recipe but makes a great take-along bar to eat any time of the day. It's worth making—really!

Kitchen stuff you need:

Small bowl	Large bowl

Spoon and fork	9x13 baking pan

Measuring spoons	Measuring cups

Food you need:

- **2 cups old-fashioned oatmeal (rolled oats)**
- **2 cups bran flakes cereal, crushed**
- **¹/₂ cup raisins**
- **¹/₄ cup shredded coconut**
- **³/₄ cup dried cranberries**
- **¹/₂ cup salted nuts or peanuts**
- **¹/₄ cup flour**
- **¹/₂ teaspoon cinnamon**
- **2 eggs**
- **¹/₂ cup honey**
- **¹/₃ cup oil**
- **¹/₃ cup brown sugar**
- **1 tablespoon butter**

Now do something:

1. Turn the oven on to 375 degrees. In the large bowl, combine the oatmeal, bran flakes, raisins, coconut, cranberries, nuts, flour, and cinnamon. Stir it all together well.

2. Break the eggs into the small bowl and beat them well with a fork. Add the honey, oil, and brown sugar to the eggs.

3. Now put the stuff in the small bowl into the large bowl and mix the two bowls of stuff together.

4. Grease the 9x13 pan by rubbing a little butter in the pan with clean fingers or a piece of waxed paper. Press the mixture into the greased pan.

5. Bake for 20-25 minutes. Take them out of the oven and let them set for 5 minutes—then cut into bars. (Turn off the oven!) Let them cool before you wrap each one separately to take with you. Makes 20 bars.

Power Bar Checklist

 Time: This is a real baking-type recipe. It will take about 1 hour. But aren't you proud of yourself?

 Washing Dishes: The bowls are easy to wash. Just do it.

 Leftovers: This was made to be leftovers. Wrap each power bar in plastic wrap. They don't have to be refrigerated, but it may keep them a bit fresher. They will keep for 2 or 3 weeks in or out of the fridge.

 Cost: Dried fruit and nuts are kind of expensive, but they are worth it. This whole batch costs about $6.50, or about 32 cents per bar.

Chocolate Oatmeal Drop Cookies Checklist

 Time: If you have all of the ingredients on hand it will only take about 20 minutes to make these awesome cookies. They will need to set for a couple of hours before they travel well, however.

 Washing Dishes: Just the saucepan and the spoon. You may want to eat what is left on the edges of the saucepan before you wash it. Of course, that will make it easier to clean.

 Leftovers: You can keep the cookies in the refrigerator or on the shelf in a covered container for about a week. Sometimes they crumble a little after a couple of days, but you probably won't have them that long anyway.

Cost: The entire batch costs about $1.45. That's about 5 cents each. Oh yes, you can eat lots!

Chocolate Oatmeal Drops

These cookies are no-bake and taste great. These little gems travel well—but you'll probably eat them before lunch anyway.

Kitchen stuff you need:

Saucepan | Spoon

Aluminum foil | Measuring cups

Food you need:
2 cups sugar
1/3 cup cocoa
1/2 cup milk
1/2 cup butter
1 cup shredded coconut
3 cups old-fashioned oatmeal
(rolled oats)

1 Now do something:

Measure the sugar and put it in the saucepan. Measure the cocoa and stir it all together. Stir it until there aren't any lumps.

2 Now add the milk and butter. The butter will look funny because it isn't melted. That's okay, it will melt in a minute. Set the pan on the stove on medium heat and stir the mixture until all the sugar is dissolved. Let it come to a boil. (The mixture is kind of thick so it sort of pops when it boils.) Only let it boil for 1 minute, stirring all the time.

3 Take it off the stove and add the coconut and rolled oats. (Don't forget to turn off the stove!) Stir it all up until it is well mixed.

4 Make little mounds of individual cookies on the foil using a spoon. (See page 176 to see how big to make them.) The cookies will be sticky, but they will set up as they harden. It will take about 2 or 3 hours before they are completely set. This makes a lot of cookies—about 30 or so. You'll be glad you made so many!

Take Along Tips

You are always going somewhere. Whether it is to class, to a meeting, to a party, or just to hang out with friends, take your food along with you. It will save you money, time, and will taste better than fast food you pick up along the way. Here are a few ideas for packing food when you are on the go.

- Empty a little water out of a plastic bottle of water and keep it in the freezer. After it freezes, use it to keep your food cold when you take it with you. Plus, you'll have a nice cool bottle of water to drink later in the day.

- If you take your lunch often (you have a 12:00 class!) make it the night before and have it ready to go in the morning. That way your morning will go more smoothly and you won't be starving and crabby by 2:00.

- Be sure and have a small cooler or cooler sack on hand for those times when you really need to keep foods hot or cold—like for tailgating or other outdoor activities.

- For daily lunches, try to take things with you that won't spoil if they get too hot or cold. Unless you are super-organized or like only a few lunch-type items, you don't have time to worry about if the food is spoiling.

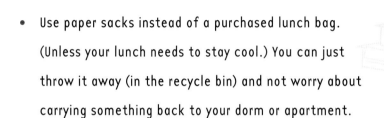

- Use paper sacks instead of a purchased lunch bag. (Unless your lunch needs to stay cool.) You can just throw it away (in the recycle bin) and not worry about carrying something back to your dorm or apartment.

- Always throw away any lunchtime or carry-along leftovers after you are done eating. By the time you take it back to where you live, it will no doubt be mushy, smashed, or spoiled.

- Carry a water bottle and refill it instead of buying new bottles of water every time you want a drink. Wash the bottle often, however, because it can breed bacteria.

- If you meet someone for lunch, take turns bringing the lunch. Unless they are a rotten cook.

Read the Box

Packaged and boxed products are so convenient. There are brownie mixes, packaged waffles, tubes of biscuits, boxes of corn bread mix, and just about everything else you can imagine. But by adding your own special touch to these convenience products you can make them even better—and you can claim the good taste is all your doing!

just add
water!

NUTRITION

vitamins...0%

protein...0%

fiber...0%

healthy stuff...0%

calories...100%

Triple Fudge
Brownie Mix

cake
mix

STATISTICS 1

STATISTICS 2

essay notes

how to study last minute

WORKBOOK B

WORKBOOK A

ORGANIC CHEMISTRY

Peanut Butter Brownies

The combined flavors of peanut butter and chocolate get even better when they are baked together in the same pan!

Kitchen stuff you need:

Large bowl	Spoon

Table knife	8x8-inch baking pan

Measuring cups

Food you need:

Brownie mix in a box (to fill an 8x8-inch pan)
(Egg, water, and whatever else the box tells you to use)
$\frac{1}{2}$ cup peanut butter

Now do something:

1 Preheat the oven to whatever the mix tells you to do—probably 350 degrees. Mix the brownie mix just like it tells you to on the box.

2 Pour it into the square pan.

3 Using a spoon, drop the peanut butter by teaspoonfuls on six different spots on top of the brownie batter.

4 Use the knife to make lines through the batter, slightly mixing in the peanut butter. Don't mix it too much.

5 Bake as directed on the brownie box. Let it cool for just a minute before you cut the brownies. Yes, it is hard to wait. Makes 12 small brownies.

Peanut Butter Brownies Checklist

Time: From the time you open the box to the time you are eating these little gems, it will be about 45 minutes.

Washing Dishes: You only have the bowl, spoon, and pan they are baked in. Wash that pan right away or at least put some water in it.

Leftovers: Take the brownies out of the pan and put them in a covered container. They should keep for about 5 days. They will keep best in the refrigerator. You can freeze them for up to 3 months.

Cost: Depending on the kind of brownie mix you buy, about $1.25 for the whole pan.

Peanut Butter 101
(answers on page 187)

1. Yea for peanut butter! Where did it begin?
A. Africa B. China C. In America, during the Civil War

2. Who developed peanut butter?
A. Peter Pan B. A kid named Skippy
C. Kellogg brothers

3. Who's the father of the peanut industry?
A. Jimmy Carter B. Mr. Peanut
C. George Washington Carver

4. Instead of PB&J sandwiches, what celebrity loved fried peanut butter and banana sandwiches?
A. Mick Jagger B. Elvis C. Ringo Star

Sugar and Spice Biscuits Checklist

 Time: You can be eating these treats in about 30 minutes from the time you open the tube.

 Washing Dishes: The dishes are easy to do because you used lots of butter!

 Leftovers: There probably won't be any, but you can keep these unrefrigerated for about 2 or 3 days. Warm them up in the microwave for a few seconds and they'll taste better.

 Cost: Depending on what you spend for the biscuits (prices vary a lot by brand), each half sugary biscuit costs about a dime. Yeah, it's worth it.

Great with milk!

Sugar and Spice Biscuits

Grab a glass of milk or orange juice and start eating these sugary treats—you won't be able to stop!

Kitchen stuff you need:

8x8 inch baking pan	Knife
Spoon	Two small bowls
Measuring spoons	Measuring cups

Food you need:
- 1/2 cup sugar
- 2 teaspoons cinnamon
- 1 tube purchased refrigerated biscuits
- 1/4 cup butter

Now do something:

1 Turn on the oven to 375 degrees or whatever the tube of biscuits tells you to do.

2 In the first small bowl, mix the sugar and the cinnamon. In the second small bowl (microwave-safe), melt the butter in the microwave for 20 seconds.

3 Open the tube of biscuits. Be careful, it is always a surprise when they pop open! Take them out of the tube and cut the biscuits in half with the knife. Dip each half biscuit first in the butter and then in the sugar cinnamon mixture. Lay them in the pan so they overlap a little. They should all fit.

4 Read the Box

Put the biscuits in the oven and bake for about 20 minutes or until they are just turning golden brown. Take out of the oven. Eat while warm just as they are or add a little jelly, peanut butter, or honey. Makes twice as many biscuits as there are in the can because you cut them in half. That is just good math.

Double Chicken Noodle Soup

Combine some simple stuff together to make this flavorful soup.

Kitchen stuff you need:

Can opener

Large bowl

Spoon

Measuring cups

Food you need:

- 1 $10^3/_4$-oz. can condensed chicken noodle soup
- 2 cans water
- 2 1.8-oz packets dry cup-size noodle soup mix
- $^1/_2$ cup frozen peas

Now do something:

1 Open the can of soup. Pour it into the microwave-safe bowl. Add the 2 cans of water.

2 Open the dry noodle packets. Pour them into the bowl with the soup and water. Don't add any more water.

3 Add the peas. Mix everything together.

4 Put the bowl in the microwave and cook on high heat about 5 minutes or until the soup bubbles. You will probably need to stir it once during that 5 minutes. Makes 3 servings. You won't believe how good this is!

Double Chicken Noodle Soup Checklist

 Time: From the time you open the can and packets to the minute you sit down to taste this warm and satisfying soup, it should be about 15 minutes. Add some crackers and cheese and you have a meal!

 Washing Dishes: There is only the bowl and spoon. It is a super-easy clean up so just do it.

 Leftovers: Keep the leftover soup in a covered container in the refrigerator. It will keep for up to 3 days. Throw it away after that.

Cost: The total cost of the entire batch of soup is about $1.30, or about 40 cents per serving.

Other stuff you can add to your soup:

- 1 small can drained corn
- 2 tablespoons chopped red pepper
- 1/4 cup cubed, cooked ham or cooked turkey
- Crackers of any kind, of course

Corny Corn Bread Checklist

 Time: If you have everything you need, it will take about 45 minutes to make this delicious corn bread.

 Washing Dishes: There are quite a few items to wash but they are all easy to do. No big deal here.

 Leftovers: Keep the leftover corn bread in the refrigerator for up to 2 days. You can warm it in the microwave.

 Cost: If you use a value-priced corn muffin mix and happen to get the corn on sale you can make the entire batch of corn bread for about $1.00. That means only about 12 cents per serving. If you add jelly, honey, or gobs of butter, then plan for a few cents more.

Try a little honey on top!

Corny Corn Bread

You'll be surprised how you won't want to stop eating this corny combination.

Kitchen stuff you need:

Large bowl

Can opener

Fork

Measuring cups

Measuring spoons

Spoon

8x8-inch baking pan

Food you need:

1 9-oz. box corn muffin mix
1 15¼-oz. can whole kernel corn
1 egg
½ cup milk
1 tablespoon butter

Now do something:

1 Turn on the oven to 400 degrees. Open the box of corn muffin mix and pour it into the bowl. (Don't follow the directions on the box.)

2 Open the can of corn and drain off the liquid into the sink. You can use a strainer or just carefully pour out the liquid. (See page 159 for tips on how to drain veggies.) Be careful and don't lose the corn with it. Pour the corn into the bowl with the muffin mix.

3 Crack the egg into a cup or dish and beat it up with a fork. Add the beaten egg to the corn bread mixture. Now add the milk and mix up the batter well.

4 Read the Box

4 Grease the pan with the butter. (See page 160 for tips on greasing pans.) Pour the batter into the pan and bake for about 20 minutes or until it is done. (See how to test to see if it is done on page 161.) Cut and serve warm with butter. You can also add jelly, honey, peanut butter, or syrup. Makes 9 large servings.

Cherry Chocolate Cupcakes

Impress your friends with these brownie-like cupcakes with cherries inside. Decorate each one with a candy treat.

Kitchen stuff you need:

Cupcake/muffin tin

Cupcake liners

Large bowl

Spoon

Can opener

Knife

Fork

Food you need:

1 box Devil's Food cake mix

3 eggs

1 21-oz. can cherry pie filling

No-stick cooking spray such as Pam (if you are not using liners)

Purchased canned chocolate frosting

Candy that you like

Now do something:

1
Turn on the oven to 350 degrees. Put the dry cake mix in the bowl. Don't follow the directions on the box!

2
Crack the eggs into a cup or dish and beat them up with a fork. Add them to the dry cake mix. Stir with the spoon. Keep mixing until it is blended really well. You shouldn't see any dry mix after you are done stirring.

3
Open the pie filling and add it all to the cake mixture. Stir it up well.

4
Put the paper cupcake liners in the pan if you want to use them. Cupcake liners make cleaning the pan a lot easier! If you want to put the batter directly into the muffin tin that

is fine, too. Just be sure to grease the muffin tins with a little no-stick cooking spray. Fill each cupcake liner or greased cup about ⅔ full. You will use only half the batter for the first 12 cupcakes. (Because this recipe makes 24 cupcakes, you will bake one batch and then let the pan cool and bake another batch.)

Put the cupcakes in the oven and bake for about 20 minutes or until a toothpick comes out clean when you put it in and pull it out. (See page 161 for baking tips).

Take the cupcakes out of the oven and let them cool. Use a table knife to frost each cupcake with any canned chocolate frosting that you like. Put a candy on top to make it look cool. Makes 24 cupcakes.

Cherry Chocolate Cupcakes Checklist

 Time: It will take about 40 minutes before you get to eat a nice, warm cherry chocolate cupcake.

 Washing Dishes: If you use cupcake liners, and the muffin tin stays clean, then all you have to wash is the bowl and utensils. If you put the batter directly in the greased cups, use a scrubber to wash the muffin tin well.

 Leftovers: Keep the extra cupcakes in the refrigerator because of the cherry stuff inside. They will keep better that way.

 Cost: The 24 cupcakes cost about $2.20. That's less than 10 cents each!

Egg Casserole

This takes a little planning, but it is so worth it. You won't believe how good this tastes!

Kitchen stuff you need:

8x8-inch baking pan

Large bowl

Fork

Measuring cups

Aluminum foil

Food you need:

No-stick cooking spray such as Pam

$\frac{1}{2}$ package frozen waffles (about 8 or 9 squares)

$1\frac{1}{2}$ cup shredded cheddar cheese

6 eggs

1 cup milk

$\frac{3}{4}$ cup chopped ham

1 Now do something:

Grease the pan with cooking spray. Lay the first layer of waffles (about $\frac{1}{3}$ of the package) in the bottom of the pan. If they don't fit, break them in half making a single layer of waffles. Sprinkle $\frac{1}{3}$ of the cheese on the waffles.

2 Break the eggs one at a time into a cup or dish. Put them in the bowl and beat them with the fork. Add the milk. Mix it all together. Pour about $\frac{1}{3}$ of the mixture over the waffles and cheese. Add $\frac{1}{2}$ of the chopped ham.

3 Add another layer of waffles. Add more cheese, ham, and egg mixture. Continue layering until the top layer is waffles. Add a final sprinkle of cheese. Be sure that you use all of the egg mixture.

4 Cover with foil and put in the fridge overnight. If you can't wait that long, at least let it set in the fridge for 3 hours. The waffles need to soak up the liquid.

5 Turn the oven to 350 degrees. Take the casserole out of the fridge and bake with the foil on for about 45 minutes or until there isn't any liquid and the top is getting slightly golden brown. Take it out of the oven and let it stand for about 5 or 10 minutes before you cut it. Wow—you'll love this! It makes 9 small servings.

Egg Casserole Checklist

Time: Well, if you count letting it set in the fridge overnight, this takes a long time. If you count the actual putting together of it, about 20 minutes to prepare and 45 minutes to bake. Whatever the case, it is worth it.

Washing Dishes: Lots of cups and spoons and stuff—but all are really easy to wash. After you put the leftovers in a covered container, the big pan you baked it in may take a little longer. Soak it if you can't get to it right away.

Leftovers: You can keep the leftover egg casserole in a covered container in the fridge for up to 3 days. It warms up well in the microwave.

Cost: The total cost for the casserole is about $3.45. That is about 38 cents per serving.

Lemon Cake

Add a few sprinkles to make this cake a party cake!

Kitchen stuff you need:

Large bowl	Spoon, fork
8x8-inch cake pan	Measuring spoons
Two small bowls	Measuring cups

Food you need:

No-stick cooking spray such as Pam

1 9-oz. box white cake mix

(Egg, water, and whatever else the box tells you to use)

1 lemon

1 tablespoon butter

1 cup powdered sugar

Colored sprinkles (optional)

Now do something:

1 Grease the cake pan with the cooking spray. Mix up the cake following the instructions on the box. Make it just like it says and put it into the greased 8x8-inch cake pan. Bake the cake according to the directions on the box.

2 While the cake is baking, make the lemon glaze. First cut the lemon in half and squeeze out the juice into one of the small bowls. Be sure there aren't any seeds in the juice. (See page 159 for tips on squeezing lemons.)

3 Melt the butter in the other microwave-safe small bowl in the microwave for about 20 seconds. Add this to the lemon juice. Add the powdered sugar and beat with the spoon until it is smooth. If it is too thick, add a little water. You want the glaze to be about the consistency of thick cream.

4 When the cake is done, take it out of the oven. Use the fork to make holes in the top of the cake. Stick the fork in the cake about 8-10 times all over the top.

5 Pour the glaze over the warm cake. Add sprinkles if you like. Cool slightly before serving. Makes 9 servings.

Lemon Cake Checklist

 Time: To bake the cake and add the impressive glaze—about an hour.

 Washing Dishes: There are lots of utensils, but the lemon juice will make the dishes cleaner. Really! (See tips on cleaning, page 171.)

Leftovers: Hopefully you won't eat the whole cake. (Ask friends over to help you eat it!) Keep the leftover cake in the refrigerator in a covered container for up to 3 days. It will get pretty moist and soggy after that.

 Cost: Cake mix is cheap. We bought our small-size mix for 38 cents. Lemons vary a lot in price depending on time of year. An average cost for the entire cake is about 75 cents.

Tips on Using Packaged Items

There are so many great convenience products to buy, and they can save you time. Just check out these tips before you fill the cart with only products that come in a box.

- Compare prices of convenience box products and the cost of making it yourself "from scratch". Many times boxed cake mixes and brownie mixes are less expensive than if you bought all of the ingredients you need to make the item.

- Look at the ingredients in the mix. Everyone needs to watch what chemicals and additives are in any product. Watch out for long lists of preservatives and colored dyes. Of course, oftentimes there needs to be some preservatives, but you don't need too much of a good thing.

- Many times coupons you receive as a student or get in the mail are for new convenience products. Even though it may look like a new, fun thing to try, be sure it is really a bargain. If so, then that is the time to try it.

- When you are following the directions on the convenience box, be sure to keep the box until the food you are making is done.

Sometimes there are directions on the box that you might need even after it is in the oven. Looking for the box in the garbage is not much fun!

- Some convenience products are much cheaper if you buy them in larger package sizes, such as frozen waffles. If you do buy the larger size to save money, just use what you need and then be sure to put the rest away in the freezer or fridge to use later. Buying a larger quantity of items that you can't use later (like a large size tube of biscuits) wastes money.

- Always be sure the quality of the product is worth the price. Some cheap all-in-one dinners are of such poor quality you won't get the nutrients you need and the taste may not be worth it either.

Eat Your Fruits and Veggies

Yes, they are good for you. But they are also delicious and can be prepared in so many yummy ways. Sprinkled with cheese, arranged on a giant cookie, baked up with spices, or just quickly stirred together, fruit and veggies just can't be beat.

Time: This really-good-for-you treat only takes about 15 minutes if you have all of the stuff you need.

 Washing Dishes: There aren't very many. The utensils are easy to wash.

 Leftovers: You can keep the apples in the fridge for about 4 days in a covered container. Just microwave for a few seconds to warm them up if you want to. Add a scoop of ice cream for a great dessert.

 Cost: Depending if you pick the apples off of a tree or buy them, this is a really inexpensive recipe—less than 50 cents a serving.

Apples 101
(answers on page 187)

 1. Apples are grown in all 50 states.
A. True   B. False

 2. A medium apple has how many calories?
A. 10   B. 80   C. 300

 3. Apples belong to which scientific family?
A. Rosaceae   B. Appleala   C. The Smiths

 4. The apple blossom is the state flower of
A. Michigan.   B. Alaska.   C. Rhode Island.

Awesome Baked Apples

Warm and spicy apples—and you did it yourself in your microwave!

Kitchen stuff you need:

Small bowl	Sharp knife

Measuring cups	Measuring spoons

Food you need:
2 medium apples
2 tablespoons sugar
1 teaspoon cinnamon
½ cup water

1 **Now do something:**
Wash the apples.

2 Cut the apples in half and take out the core. (See page 158 for tips on cutting up apples.) Now slice each of those halves into 4 pieces. You'll have 8 pieces for each apple—a total of 16 slices. (Wow, that math did help you.) Place them in the small microwave-safe bowl, overlapping the slices if you need to.

3 Mix the sugar, cinnamon, and water together in a cup. Pour it over the apples.

4 Place the bowl of apples in the microwave and cook on high for 5 minutes or until the apples are tender.

5 Eat while hot or refrigerate and eat them cold later. Makes 2 servings. Yum.

5 Eat Your Fruits and Veggies!

Cabbage Salad

This salad is going to be your favorite—if you like cabbage and oranges.
Maybe even if you don't!

Kitchen stuff you need:

| Large bowl | Spoon |

Measuring cups

Food you need:
1 bag shredded cabbage
1 8-oz. can mandarin
   oranges, drained
$\frac{1}{2}$ cup whole almonds
1 package Ramen
   noodles (dry,
   uncooked)
$\frac{1}{2}$ cup Italian dressing

1

Now do something:
   Open the bag of cabbage and put it in the bowl. The bag should say that the cabbage has been washed. If not, wash it first by putting it in a strainer and then rinsing it. Let it drain until the water is all out.

2

Drain the oranges. (See page 159 for tips on draining fruits from a can.) Throw the juice away. Add the oranges to the cabbage. Now add the almonds. Stir it all together and mix together well.

3

Break up the uncooked Ramen noodles into little chunks and add to the mixture. (Don't use the seasoning packet.) You can leave some in larger pieces than others. Break the uncooked noodles into pieces about the size of a quarter.

4

Add the Italian dressing. Stir until it is all moistened. Eat right away. Makes enough for 6 hungry people.

Cabbage Salad Checklist

 Time: If you have all of the ingredients on hand, this will take about 15 minutes to make.

 Washing Dishes: This is really easy. All you have to wash is the bowl that the salad is made in and the spoon.

 Leftovers: This doesn't keep very well, so only make what you will eat. The salad gets soggy very quickly. But you can keep the shredded cabbage and oranges in separate containers in the refrigerator for about 3 or 4 days and mix the other ingredients in when you want to have the salad.

Cost: The whole cabbage salad costs about $2.40 so each serving is about 40 cents.

Eat lots—it's good for you!

Mexican Salad Crisps

Okay, so you can go buy the salad shells—but these are so-o-o-o much cheaper and fun to make.

Kitchen stuff you need:

2 small bowls | Cookie sheet

Custard cups or oven-safe bowls

Food you need:

Purchased flour tortillas
No-stick cooking
   spray such as Pam

Stuff to put in the Salad Crisps like:

Lettuce, cheese, sour cream, chiles, ripe olives, refried beans, salsa, cooked ground beef or chicken

1 Now do something:

Heat the oven to 400 degrees.

2 Note: Tortillas come in more than one size. Purchase small tortillas for small bowls and large ones for large bowls. Spray the no-stick cooking spray on both sides of the tortilla. Place the tortilla between the two upside-down custard cups or small oven-proof bowls. (Be VERY SURE the bowls are ovenproof.) Fold the tortilla shell, if needed, to fit. The second bowl won't fit tightly over the tortilla, it will just help keep its shape.

3 Place the bowls and tortilla on the baking sheet and place in oven. Bake for 3 minutes. Use a potholder to take it out of

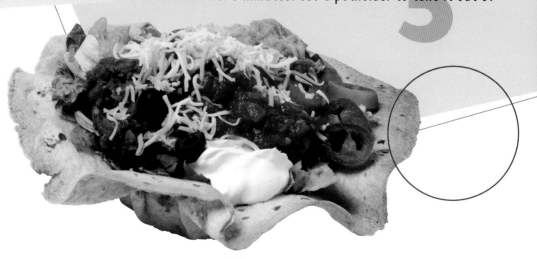

the oven and also to take off the top bowl. Put the cookie sheet back in the oven and bake the tortilla 4 more minutes draped over just one bowl. Take the cookie sheet out of the oven (again, use the potholder!) and let the shell cool. Take it off of the other bowl. You just made a cool salad crisp! (You can make more than one in the oven at a time.)

Now you are ready to fill the totally edible salad holder with whatever you like on your salad. Try shredded or chopped lettuce, black olives, green chiles, refried beans, sour cream, Monterey Jack cheese, salsa, or anything else you love. Eat right away.

Mexican Salad Crisps Checklist

 Time: The crispy salad holders only take a few minutes. Creating your masterpiece of a salad may take a little longer.

 Washing Dishes: Just wash the two bowls and the cookie sheet. You'll eat the salad holder.

 Leftovers: The shells will keep in a sealed plastic bag for a few days. The shells filled with salad need to be eaten right away.

 Cost: The shells cost pennies to make. What you put in them is up to you.

Sweet Fruit Salad

There's nothing like a little fruit and some marshmallows to make you feel light and healthy!

Kitchen stuff you need:

Sharp knife

Spoon

Large bowl

Measuring cups

Food you need:
2 cups cut up mixed fruit
Choose from:
Strawberries, apples
raspberries, fresh or
   canned pineapple,
   grapes, bananas, kiwi,
   and blueberries
¹/₂ cup small
   marshmallows
¹/₂ cup shredded coconut
1 cup whipped non-dairy
   topping such as Cool
   Whip

1

Now do something:

Wash all of the fruit that you plan to use. You don't have to wash bananas. If you are using canned pineapple, be sure and drain the juice from the can before you use the fruit. (For tips on draining fruits, see page 159.) You can save the leftover juice and pineapple in a covered container and keep it in the fridge to eat later.

2

Cut up the fruit and put it in the bowl. Cut the grapes and strawberries in half. Be sure to peel the kiwi and then slice it. (For tips on cutting up fruit, see page 159.) You can cut the fruit into bite-size pieces or leave the pieces larger. Note: Don't choose citrus fruits such as oranges or grapefruit because they will curdle the non-dairy topping.

3

Add the marshmallows, coconut, and the whipped non-dairy topping. Mix it all together. Eat right away. Makes 4 large servings.

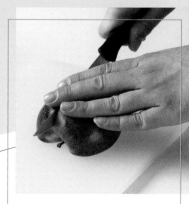

Time: Cutting up fruit takes time. Allow about 20 minutes to make it right.

Washing Dishes: Just the knives, spoon, and bowl you mix it in—no big deal.

Leftovers: This doesn't keep very well. If you plan to keep it for a day or two, don't use bananas. They will turn a nasty-looking brown and you won't want to eat it anyway. Otherwise, it will keep for about a day.

Cost: This really depends on the fruit that you choose. If a fruit is in season, it will be cheaper. You should be able to make this salad for about $2.00 or 50 cents per serving.

Put it on a fancy plate!

5 Eat Your Fruits and Veggies!

Veggie Quesadillas

Two tortillas, some cheese, and whatever else you like and you are good to go!

Kitchen stuff you need:

Paper towel | Sharp knife

Measuring cups

Food you need:
2 flour tortillas
¹/₂ cup shredded cheese
(cheddar, co-jack, taco
**   flavored or whatever**
**   kind you like)**
Chopped red and
**   green peppers**
Salsa

Now do something:

1   Lay one of the tortillas on the paper towel. Tortillas come in all kinds of flavors and sizes. Choose what you like.

2   Sprinkle the cheese on the tortilla. Add the chopped peppers.

3   Put the other tortilla on top of the mixture. Carefully lift the two tortillas on the paper towel and put it in the microwave. Cook on high for about 30 seconds or until the cheese is melted.

4   Cutting the quesadilla is what makes it cool. (A pizza cutter works well if you have one!) Cut it like a pizza and serve immediately with salsa. You can probably eat the whole thing yourself. Otherwise, it serves 2.

Veggie Quesadillas Checklist

 Time: From tortilla to quesadilla is about 10 minutes.

 Washing Dishes: This is so easy. You throw away the paper towel and wash the knife.

 Leftovers: Quesadillas don't keep very well. Make just what you are going to eat or serve. The tortillas will keep for a long time (at least 2 weeks) if they are in the refrigerator.

Cost: Depending on what you put in the quesadilla the cost varies a lot. For what we used, about 40 cents for the entire quesadilla or 20 cents per serving.

Other things to put on your quesadilla:

- Fresh, sliced mushrooms
- Cooked meat such as chicken, sausage, or hamburger
- Black olives
- Green olives
- Green chiles
- Drained pineapple
- Anchovies

Fruit Pizza Checklist

 Time: Cutting up fruit takes the most time. Allow about 30 minutes to make it right.

 Washing Dishes: Just the utensils and the cookie sheet. Easy.

 Leftovers: This doesn't keep very well. You'll need to eat it or serve it the same day. The crust will get soft and mushy.

 Cost: This really depends on the fruit that you choose. With the fruit that we used, one fruit pizza cost about $3.00.

Take a picture of your artful creation!

Fruit Pizza

This is so pretty—but go ahead and eat it anyway!

Kitchen stuff you need:

Cookie sheet | Sharp knife

Aluminum foil | Measuring cups

Food you need:

- ½ tube or package of ready-to-bake sugar cookie dough
- ½ cup cream cheese
- 2 cups sliced mixed fresh or canned fruit

Choose from: Strawberries, kiwi, raspberries, fresh or canned pineapple, bananas, blueberries, or whatever you like

Now do something:

1. Preheat the oven to 375 degrees. (Or whatever it says on the cookie dough package.) Open the tube of sugar cookie dough and cut in in half. You will be using only half of the dough. Put the rest back in the fridge for making cookies later—or make two pizzas.

2. Cover the cookie sheet with foil. Lay the dough on the foil and with your clean hands, pat the dough into a circle about 7 inches in diameter. (See page 177 to see this size.)

3. Put in the oven and bake for about 7 minutes or until it is just getting brown. Take it out of the oven and let it cool. Shut off the oven.

4. Spread the cream cheese on the cooled cookie crust.

5. Wash all of the fruit you are planning to use. If you are using canned fruit such as pineapple, be sure to drain it. (See page 159 for hints on draining fruit.)

6. Arrange the fruit in an artful way. For you design majors, this is the most fun part. For you engineering majors, the order does not have to be consistent. Makes 3 or 4 servings.

5 Eat Your Fruits and Veggies!

Carrot Casserole

Nothing better for you than carrots—and the cheese and onions just make it yummy!

Kitchen stuff you need:

Small bowl

Sharp knife

Measuring spoons

Measuring cups

Food you need:

- ¹/₂ of 1-lb. bag baby carrots (about 24 baby carrots)
- ¹/₂ cup water
- 1 teaspoon dried onion or 1 tablespoon chopped fresh onion
- 3 1-inch cubes of processed cheese such as Velveeta
- ¹/₂ cup cornflakes, crushed
- 1 tablespoon butter

Now do something:

1 Open the bag of carrots. You really should wash them even if the bag says they are already washed. Don't use soap—just rinse with water. Cut them in half with the knife. Put half of the bag (about 24 little carrots) in the microwave-safe bowl. Put the rest back in the fridge.

2 Add the ¹/₂ cup water and onion to the carrots in the bowl or dish.

3 Cook in the microwave (uncovered) for about 5 minutes or until the carrots are tender. Drain off about half of the water that is left.

4 Add the cheese cubes to the carrot-onion mixture. (See page 174 to see how big to cut the cheese cubes.)

Put the casserole back in the microwave and cook for 1 minute or until the cheese is melted. Take it out of the microwave and stir it up. Put it back in the microwave and cook for 1 more minute. Take it out of the microwave.

Crush the cornflakes slightly with your clean hands and add them to the top of the casserole. Spread them around on top of the carrots until they are covered. Cut the butter into little pieces and put on top of the cornflakes. Put it back in the microwave for about 30 seconds or just until the butter is melted. Eat right away. Makes 2 servings.

Carrot Casserole Checklist

 Time: Allow about 20 minutes to make this yummy casserole.

 Washing Dishes: Just the utensils and bowl you cook it in. Pretty easy.

 Leftovers: You can keep this covered in the refrigerator for about two days. Just reheat it in the microwave.

Cost: If you get a good deal on the carrots, about 50 cents for the 2 servings. That would be a quarter for each delicious and healthy serving.

Yogurt Smoothie

Grab the blender and throw in your favorite stuff—you can eat this and study (or talk on the phone) at the same time.

Kitchen stuff you need:

Blender

Spoon

Sharp Knife

Measuring cups

Food you need:

3 strawberries or
¼ cup raspberries
½ banana
½ cup milk
1 container strawberry
yogurt
3 or 4 ice cubes or
½ cup crushed ice

1 Now do something:

Wash the fruit that you plan to use. You don't have to wash the banana. Cut up the fruit and put it in the blender. (For tips on cutting up fruit, see page 159.)

2 Add the yogurt and the milk. Push it down with a spoon if necessary. Take out the spoon. Turn on the blender and mix well. Add the ice. (If you are using ice cubes, be sure they aren't too big. If they are really large or your blender is small, put them in a sealed heavy plastic bag and hit them with a hammer to make crushed ice.)

3 Turn the blender on again and blend until it is smooth—thus the name! Makes 1 serving.

Yogurt Smoothie Checklist

 Time: Cutting up the fruit takes the most time—which isn't long. Allow about 15 minutes to make a smoothie.

 Washing Dishes: Just the blender. To clean that well, put warm water and just a drop of dish soap in the blender. Turn it on. Throw that soapy water out and rinse well.

 Leftovers: This doesn't keep very well at all in the fridge. You can freeze it in plastic cups and eat it later that way if you don't finish it all.

Cost: Depends on the fruit that you choose and what you have to pay for the yogurt. For what we used, about 60 cents.

Yogurt 101

(answers on page 187)

 1. How can you get culture?

A. Hear classical music   B. Visit an art museum   C. Eat yogurt

 2. Yogurt starts with what ingredient before fermenting?

A. Mozzarella   B. Milk   C. Mayonnaise

 3. What leader's troops lived on yogurt?

A. George Custer   B. Genghis Khan   C. Robert E. Lee

 4. Yogurt can help which one of these?

A. Bad breath   B. Intestinal problems   C. Acne

5 Eat Your Fruits and Veggies!

Fruits and Veggies—Just the Facts

You know what they say—an apple a day keeps the doctor away. Well, guess what—research shows it's true! Fruits and veggies of all kinds are good for you, so eat up!

- When cooking vegetables, cook them for the least possible amount of time. This will allow the vegetables to keep their vitamins and minerals, and will keep them a prettier color, too.

- When choosing fruits and vegetables at the grocery store, always choose the darkest and brightest colored produce. Choose the darkest green lettuce and the brightest orange carrots. Bright, dark colors show that they contain more vitamins and minerals, and they'll probably taste better too.

- Blueberries are one of the healthiest foods you can eat. They are loaded with antioxidants which has been shown in research to help prevent cancer and other diseases. When blueberries are not in season, buy them in the freezer section and thaw them out to eat as a snack. They are great with just a little milk on top. Yum!

- Broccoli is a very healthy food. It has been proven to prevent all sorts of nasty things, like cancer and strokes. Eat it raw or cooked.

- Citrus fruits, like oranges and grapefruit, help prevent colds because of their antioxidants and give you huge doses of vitamin C. Plus they are very low in calories.

- Canned green beans are a great snack to have. They contain many nutrients, and you can eat a whole can for about 70 calories. That's a lot of beans!

- You know what they say—an apple a day keeps the doctor away. Well guess what—this is probably true! Research shows that apples do indeed help fight disease. So grab one and eat it on the way to class, and maybe keep yourself from getting sick.

- Spinach contains some unusual vitamins and minerals that really can make you stronger, just like Popeye said. It is delicious in salads or cooked. Eat it however you want and you will undoubtedly feel better!

- Sweet potatoes are a delicious food full of important nutrients. Wash and then bake a sweet potato in the oven for about an hour at 350 degrees, add some butter, and you'll have a delicious and nutritious meal.

Impress Your Friends

Sometimes just a simple yet clever idea makes a recipe seem pretty special. Whether you are throwing a party for a crowd, having a special friend over to eat with you, or just feel like making your own dinner a bit more fun, these recipes are sure to make you smile.

Lasagna

Everyone loves this dish, so impress your friends and make it!

Kitchen stuff you need:

9x13-inch baking pan

Frying pan

Spoon; fork

Small bowl

Aluminum foil

Measuring cups

Food you need:

- **1 pound ground beef**
- **1 egg**
- **2 cups shredded mozzarella cheese**
- **1 cup cottage cheese**
- **1 26-oz. jar spaghetti sauce**
- **1 box no-boil lasagna noodles**

Now do something:

1 Turn on the oven to 350 degrees. Put the ground beef into the frying pan, put it on the stove, and cook it on medium high. Add some salt and pepper if you want. Brown the hamburger in the pan, breaking it up into small pieces as you cook it. Be sure there is no pink left after it is cooked. Drain off that fat or liquid into the trash or into an empty can—not in the sink. (For tips on cooking meat, see page 153.) Set the meat aside.

2 Break the egg into the small bowl and beat it up with the fork. Add the mozzarella cheese and the cottage cheese to the egg. Mix it together. Set it aside.

3 Open up the jar or can of spaghetti sauce. Now you are ready to build your lasagna! Lasagna is made by layering the noodles, cheese mixture, ground beef, and sauce. Even

126

though you can try to make it perfectly layered, it really doesn't matter that much. Just start with the lasagna noodles and end with the noodles covered with cheese. For example, put a layer of noodles in the bottom, add some of the cheese mixture, sauce, and ground beef. Now add more noodles. Add more cheese mixture, sauce, and ground beef. Do this until everything is gone.

Cover with a piece of foil and bake in the oven for about 45 minutes or until the lasagna is bubbly and the cheese is totally melted. Take it out of the oven and let it set for about 5 minutes. Now it is ready to cut and eat! You did it! Makes about 9 generous servings.

Lasagna Checklist

Time: Allow about 1½ hours for everything.

Washing Dishes: There are quite a few here. Put water in the frying pan to soak. After the meal is over, you'll need to put the leftovers in a covered container to put in the fridge. If you aren't going to wash the baking pan right away, put water in it. Then do it first thing tomorrow.

Leftovers: This makes a big recipe. The leftovers will keep well in the fridge for 3 or 4 days. Just reheat what you will eat in the microwave. You can freeze pieces of this for later as well. It will keep in the freezer for about 1 month.

Cost: Total cost for the whole recipe is about $5.50 depending on where you shop. That would be about 60 cents per serving.

Sesame Seed Breadsticks

These are some breadsticks you may want to share with only those friends you really like a lot!

Kitchen stuff you need:

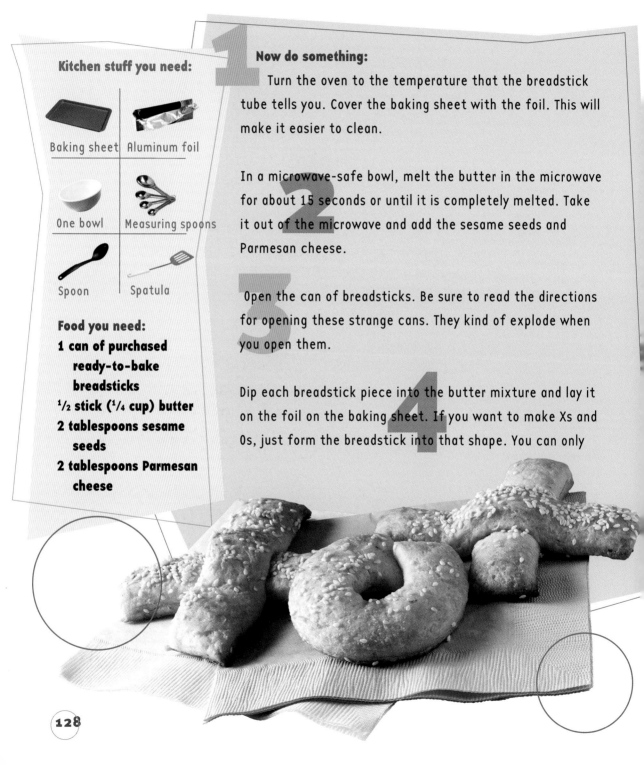

Baking sheet	Aluminum foil
One bowl	Measuring spoons
Spoon	Spatula

Food you need:

1 can of purchased ready-to-bake breadsticks
½ stick (¼ cup) butter
2 tablespoons sesame seeds
2 tablespoons Parmesan cheese

Now do something:

1 Turn the oven to the temperature that the breadstick tube tells you. Cover the baking sheet with the foil. This will make it easier to clean.

2 In a microwave-safe bowl, melt the butter in the microwave for about 15 seconds or until it is completely melted. Take it out of the microwave and add the sesame seeds and Parmesan cheese.

3 Open the can of breadsticks. Be sure to read the directions for opening these strange cans. They kind of explode when you open them.

4 Dip each breadstick piece into the butter mixture and lay it on the foil on the baking sheet. If you want to make Xs and Os, just form the breadstick into that shape. You can only make half of the can at a time on the baking sheet if you make shapes. They take up more space than if you just lay the straight pieces side by side. Bake one batch and then wait and bake the second half after the pan has cooled a bit.

5 Bake the breadsticks as directed on the can—usually about 10 minutes.

6 Remove the breadsticks from the pan using a spatula and eat right away. Makes whatever it says on the can—usually about 12 breadsticks.

Sesame Seed Breadsticks Checklist

 Time: It will take you about 30 minutes to make these rich breadsticks.

 Washing Dishes: There might seem like a lot, but none are very dirty. Do them right away or at least tonight.

 Leftovers: These will keep covered in the fridge for a day or two but they won't be as good as when they first come out of the oven.

 Cost: The can of breadsticks costs about $1.00. The sesame seeds and butter cost about 30 cents. Add it up—yup, $1.30 for all of them. It's worth it!

6 Impress Your Friends!

Fancy Yogurt Parfaits

Impress your friends with this recipe that makes you look like you are a nutrition major!

Kitchen stuff you need:

Plastic bag | Textbook

Can opener | Any clear glasses

Food you need:
- **25 vanilla wafer cookies**
- **1 container strawberry yogurt**
- **1 container blueberry yogurt**
- **1 18-oz. can fruit cocktail, drained**

Now do something:

Put the vanilla wafer cookies in a sealable plastic bag. Seal bag, expelling air from the bag. Using your least favorite textbook or other hard object, smash the cookies until they are fine crumbs.

In the bottom of each glass place a layer (about 3 tablespoons) of the crushed cookies. Next spoon on a layer of strawberry yogurt about 1/2 inch thick, and then add a 1-inch-thick layer of the fruit cocktail.

Next add a layer of blueberry yogurt, followed by a cookie layer, a strawberry yogurt layer, and a fruit layer. Eat right away. Makes 3 servings.

Time: About 15 minutes if you have the ingredients in your kitchen.

 Washing Dishes: Be sure to rinse the glasses and then you can wait a day or two if you have to, or use clear disposable glasses and you won't have any dishes!

 Leftovers: Anything leftover should be kept in the refrigerator, but these don't keep very well—they get mushy. Just make new ones if you want more.

 Cost: Each serving costs about 65 cents, depending on the size of glass that you use. Instead of using canned fruit you can use fresh fruit such as bananas, blueberries, and strawberries. Fresh fruit may cost a little more depending upon the season.

It's a party in a glass!

Caramel Corn Checklist

 Time: This takes about 15 minutes to make.

 Washing Dishes: The bowls will be sticky so put cold water in them to soak if you don't have time to do the dishes right away.

 Leftovers: Keep extra popcorn in a plastic bag—no need to refrigerate. It really is best to keep it in the freezer, if you have space, because it won't be so sticky.

 Cost: This sweet treat costs about 80 cents. That's about 20 cents per cup. You'll eat a lot.

Popcorn 101
(answers on page 187)

1. Where did popcorn first grow?
A. Mexico   B. China   C. India

2. Native Americans brought popcorn as a gift to the first Thanksgiving.
A. True   B. False

3. Where is most of the world's popcorn grown?
A. Nebraska   B. Indiana   C. New Jersey

4. What popular pastime caused popcorn consumption to decline?
A. Playing pool   B. Rollerblading   C. Watching TV

Caramel Corn

Share this gooey and sticky treat with your friends while you're studying for finals.

Kitchen stuff you need:

Large bowl | Small bowl

Measuring spoons | Spoon

Measuring cups

Food you need:
- 3 cups popped popcorn
- 1 cup honey-roasted peanuts
- 1 cup brown sugar
- 1 tablespoon milk
- ¼ cup butter
- 2 tablespoons corn syrup (look in the glossary on page 178 if you don't know what this is)

1

Now do something:

Combine the popped popcorn and peanuts in the large bowl. Stir them together. Set aside.

2

Put the brown sugar, milk, butter, and corn syrup into the small bowl. Put the bowl in the microwave for about 2 minutes or until it bubbles.

3

Take it out of the microwave and pour it over the popcorn and peanuts. Stir it up. Let it cool for a minute or two (if you can wait). Enjoy! Makes 4 cups.

6 Impress Your Friends!

Chocolate Chunk Cookies

Yes, these are really good cookies made from scratch. They aren't that hard to make and your friends will love you!

Kitchen stuff you need:

 Large bowl   Spoon

 Cookie sheet   Spatula

Measuring spoons   Measuring cups

Food you need:
1 cup (2 sticks) butter
1½ cups brown sugar
2 eggs
2½ cups flour
1 teaspoon baking soda
2 chocolate bars broken into chunks (about 1 cup of chunks)

1 **Now do something:**
Turn on the oven to 350 degrees. Take the butter out of the fridge, unwrap it, and put it in the bowl. Let the butter soften in the bowl while you study or play Nintendo. Or, if you are in a hurry, and the bowl is microwave-safe, put it in the microwave for just a few seconds to soften—not too long or it will melt to a liquid state. (Physics majors will understand this easily.)

2 After the butter is soft, add the sugar and mix it with the butter until smooth. Then add the eggs and mix again. Mix it really well.

3 Now add the flour and baking soda. Mix it again. Finally, add the broken up chocolate bars and mix it up. Now you are ready to put the dough on the baking sheet.

Using a spoon or your fingers, put 12 globs of dough each about the size of a ping-pong ball on the baking sheet. (See page 176 to see how big to make the cookies on the pan.) That means, to be efficient, you need 4 rows with 3 globs in each row. (Not all the dough will fit on the cookie sheet.) Put the cookies in the oven and bake for about 10 minutes. Take them out and use the spatula to take them off the pan and put on a sheet of foil to cool. You just made real cookies!

Let the pan cool for a few minutes and then use the rest of the dough to make more cookies until all the dough is gone. Makes about 24 cookies.

Chocolate Chunk Cookies Checklist

Time: You'll be eating warm cookies about 30 minutes from the time the butter is softened.

Washing Dishes: There will be a few, but it will be worth it. Do them right away or it could get ugly.

Leftovers: Keep the cookies in a plastic bag for up to a week. You can keep them longer but they get stale. You can put them in a plastic bag and keep in the freezer for about a month. Just take one out when you want one. They thaw very quickly.

Cost: Each cookie costs about 15 cents.

Chocolate-Covered Crispy Balls

Show your friends your artistic talent by giving each of these handmade treats a little touch of stylish chocolate.

Kitchen stuff you need:

Large bowl

Measuring cups

Plastic bag

Muffin pan

Food you need:

No-stick cooking spray
such as Pam
¼ cup butter
1 10 oz.-package big
marshmallows
6 cups crispy rice cereal
such as Rice Krispies
½ cup chocolate chips

Aluminum foil (optional)

Now do something:

1 Before you start, spray the bottom and the sides of each of the muffin cups with no-stick cooking spray. If you don't have a muffin pan, grease a piece of foil with the cooking spray—the foil will be your pan. Set the muffin pan or foil aside until you need it.

2 Put the butter and the marshmallows in the big bowl. Put the bowl in the microwave for about 2 minutes. The marshmallows will melt and puff up. Take it out, and stir it. Put it back in the microwave for about 1 more minute until it is all melted.

3 Take it out of the microwave and stir the marshmallows and butter together only for a few seconds. The marshmallows will deflate.

4 Quickly add the crispy rice cereal stirring it until all the cereal is covered with the marshmallow mixture. You will need to work quickly because the marshmallow mixture will begin to set up and will be hard to work with.

Cover your hands with butter and form the mixture into loose balls about the size of a tennis ball. (See page 176 to see about how big to make them.) Press the mixture into the muffin cups. (If you don't have a muffin pan, just make balls and put them on the piece of foil.) Do this until you have used up the mixture. It makes about 12 balls.

Put the chocolate chips into the plastic bag. Put in the microwave until they are melted— about 1 minute. Watch carefully, they burn really quickly.

Take the plastic bag out of the microwave and cut a tiny corner from one corner of the bag. Squeeze the melted chocolate on the top of the crispy balls drizzling the chocolate to make a design. Pretty cool, huh?

Chocolate-Covered Crispy Balls Checklist

Time: If you have everything in the kitchen, these treats will take about 15 minutes to make—unless you are really artistic and like to draw awesome stuff with chocolate.

Washing Dishes: The bowl is sticky so put cold water in it right away and it will be easier to wash later. The muffin pan will be easy because you greased it. If you used foil, just throw it away.

Leftovers: Wrap the individual treats in plastic wrap or put in plastic bags so they won't dry out. They will last for 3 or 4 days. You don't have to put them in the refrigerator.

Cost: The cereal is about 50 cents, and the marshmallows cost about $1.00. The chocolate chips you use cost about 25 cents. That means each ball costs about 15 cents. Pretty cheap treat.

Taco Cheese Dip

This rich, filling, (and yummy) dip is sure to become the one they ask for everytime you throw a party.

Kitchen stuff you need:

Frying pan | Spoon

Large bowl

Food you need:
1 **pound ground beef**
1 **15$^1/_2$-oz. jar cheese sauce**
1 **24-oz. jar picante sauce**
1 **bag of tortilla chips**

Green chiles (optional)

1 Now do something:

Put the ground beef into the frying pan. Brown the meat in the pan, breaking it up into small pieces as you cook it. Be sure there is no pink left after it is cooked. If the meat is greasy or there is a lot of liquid after it is cooked, drain off that liquid into the trash or into an empty can—not in the sink. (For tips on cooking meat, see page 153.) Put the meat into the bowl.

2 Open the jar of cheese sauce and add it to the ground beef.

3 Open the jar of picante sauce and add it to the meat mixture. Stir it all up well.

4 Put it in the microwave for about 5 minutes or until it bubbles. Stir it halfway through the cooking time. Note: This is also a good dip to put in a small slow cooker. That way it stays hot for a long time.

5 Serve with taco chips. Add some green chiles on top if you like. Makes about 12 servings.

Time: Cooking the meat takes some time, but other than that this is really quick and easy—about 20 minutes. You can keep this hot in a small slow cooker if you are having a party.

 Washing Dishes: Just the frying pan and utensils. If you use the slow cooker, be sure to put water in the pan part of the slow cooker after you put the leftovers away. That will make it easier to wash. NEVER put the slow cooker itself into the water. You can only wash the pan part. If the rest is dirty, just wipe it off.

 Leftovers: This will keep in the fridge in a covered container for 2 or 3 days. Just heat up what you will use.

Cost: The dip and chips together cost about $3.90—about 30 cents a serving.

Spiced Coffee

Who needs a fancy coffee place to get that rich flavor you love? Have this mix on hand and you'll feel like you stood in line a long time for this coffee treat.

Kitchen stuff you need:

Large bowl | Spoon

Measuring spoons | Measuring cups

Food you need:

- ¹/₂ cup instant coffee granules
- ¹/₂ cup powdered non-dairy creamer
- ¹/₃ cup sugar
- ³/₄ teaspoon ground cinnamon
- ¹/₄ teaspoon ground nutmeg
- ¹/₈ teaspoon ground cardamom (optional— but it makes it taste great!)

Now do something:

1. Measure all the ingredients and put them into the large bowl. Stir up the mixture well. Be sure all the spices, coffee, and other ingredients are thoroughly mixed up.

2. Put the mixture in a tightly covered container or plastic bag. This makes enough for about 15 cups of coffee.

3. For 1 serving, place 2 to 3 tablespoons of the coffee mix in a coffee cup or mug. Add 1 cup of steaming hot water and stir to dissolve. Relax and enjoy!

Coffee 101

(answers on page 187)

A. 1. **What is the most popular drink worldwide?**
A. Milk   B. Coffee   C. Kool-Aid

A. 2. **What American war was largely planned in a coffee house?**
A. American Revolution   B. World War II   C. War of 1812

A. 3. **If you are a girl, and you like coffee, you should move to**
A. Japan   B. Austria.   C. Turkey.

A. 4. **What caused Americans to start drinking coffee in large quantities?**
A. College   B. Lack of milk   C. Boston Tea Party

Spiced Coffee Checklist

Time: Making the mix takes about 20 minutes. Making a cup of the rich coffee to drink from the mix takes about 30 seconds.

Washing dishes: So easy—practically dust out the bowl.

Leftovers: This is made to be leftovers—will keep for up to a month or longer tightly covered.

Cost: The whole batch costs about $2.20 and makes about 15 cups of coffee—that's about 15 cents per serving.

6 Impress Your Friends!

Tips on Entertaining—
Show Them You Can Cook!

Go ahead—throw a party and have someone over. You've studied enough this week. Show off your talents and impress your friends!

- Keep it simple. If you are going to have a party and try to cook for it, remember that the point is to get together, not to fry your brain with stress. Try a few recipes that you feel comfortable with and then build from there. Start out small with a few people. Invite more next time.

- Make it easy on everyone—have a potluck. You provide the main food dish, the plates and the drinks, and let everyone else bring some food. If they all bring desserts, oh well. What's wrong with that?

- Have a plan when you organize the menu. Think how foods and flavors will compliment each other. Don't have mashed potatoes and white rice for the same meal. One starch is enough. Add a crisp green salad for crunch.

- If you have something rich for the main dish, such as lasagna, then balance it with a light dessert, such as a bowl of sherbet and cookies. Keep the drink simple like ice water, milk, or iced tea.

- Not enough dishes for a crowd? Don't panic. Use sturdy paper products and plastic utensils. Cleanup is a whole lot easier, too.

- Be sure the kitchen is clean before you invite people over. Not only will it look better, but you will be able to clean up much faster if you start with a clean kitchen. And if someone offers to stay and help clean up—let them. The more help the better!

- Of course you won't be having a fancy dinner, but just in case, always remember to serve from the left and remove from the right. That's just good to know.

Stuff You Need to Know

Since you're into this cooking thing pretty good by now, you'll need to know a few things so you continue to look professional. You need to know things about food safety, how to buy groceries, how to cook meat and vegetables, how to set the table, how to clean up and more. Yup, you guessed it, it's all in this chapter.

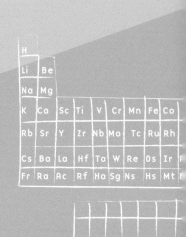

Food Safety

So you're ready to cook, but what to do first? There is no point in cooking if you aren't going to keep things safe—that means keeping things clean and uncontaminated. So first, wash your hands! All those germs you picked up in class, from friends, and who knows wherever else, need to be washed off before you start cooking. Keep your food safe—it's an absolute must!

Keep It Clean!

Basic common sense cleanliness is the best way to prevent the spread of bacteria and keep your food safe. Proper food handling is a must. Whether at the grocery store, taking food home, or fixing meals, keeping things clean will ensure that your food not only tastes great but is safe to eat. Follow these rules:

1. Wash your hands! Always, wash your hands in hot, soapy water before, during, and after cooking and eating. Wash them for at least 20 seconds. This is the No. 1 way to prevent the spread of bacteria and viruses (and prevent cold and flu), and is the best way to keep you and your food safe. If in doubt, wash your hands!

2. Keep everything that touches food clean. Bacteria can hitch rides around your kitchen on dirty utensils, sponges, dishcloths, plates, knives, and cutting boards. Use fresh towels and dishcloths at least

every other day. And always clean your cutting board or work surface with hot soapy water after each use.

3. Do NOT cross-contaminate! Keep raw meat, poultry, fish, and their juices from coming into contact with any other foods that will not be cooked. Use one cutting board for cutting raw meat and another one for cutting up vegetables and fruits.

Keep Cold Foods Cold and Hot Foods Hot!

1. Keep your refrigerator and freezer cold. Keep your refrigerator at 35–40 degrees F and your freezer at or below 0 degrees F.

2. Immediately put all meat and dairy items in the refrigerator or freezer after you buy them—never leave them in a warm car or trunk. Use roasts, steaks, and chops within 2 days if they are in the refrigerator. All chicken, turkey, ground meat, or fish should be cooked within 1 or 2 days. If you aren't going to eat it right away, freeze it. Most meats can be kept in the freezer for up to 6 months. To thaw meat, place it in the fridge on a plate or in a bag. Never just leave it on the counter to thaw. After the meat is thawed, cook it right away—within a day. Never refreeze raw meat.

3. Refrigerate cooked foods promptly after serving (within 2 hours of cooking). Store leftovers in small containers rather than large ones so they chill quickly in the fridge. Never let foods sit out after cooking because bacteria can quickly grow.

4. When reheating foods, heat thoroughly. Leftovers should be well-heated or boiled before being served again.

5. Most meat and poultry foods should be cooked until there is no red or pink color in the meat. That includes all ground meats like ground beef, ground turkey, and sausage. Beef roasts and steaks can be served with a slight pink color left in the middle if you like it that way. But the meat has to reach a certain temperature before the bacteria is killed, so don't take risks. Rotate or stir meat frequently during cooking to ensure all sides and the interior are evenly cooked, especially in the microwave, which can cook foods unevenly.

Be Sure it is Safe!

1. When preparing canned vegetables and soups, always bring them to a full boil. If using home-canned vegetables, boil for at least 20 minutes. This will kill most bacteria, some of which can be deadly. If the top is not flat on the glass canning jar or there is a bulge on a

purchased metal can, that means it is spoiled—throw it out before tasting it!

4. Never partially cook foods and then set them aside to finish cooking later. Cook your food all at one time; separating the cooking time may allow bacteria to grow.

5. Never eat undercooked eggs. Make sure both the egg white and yolk are firm and opaque, not runny and translucent.

6. Read the labels! Don't buy anything if the "sell by" date has expired. Follow the "use by" or "freeze by" dates on a package. Most dairy products are good for one week after the "sell by" date. After that, throw them out.

Food Substitutions

Sometimes you may not have just the right ingredients on hand.
Here is a handy list of things you can substitute if you are
missing an item in a recipe.

1 teaspoon baking powder = $\frac{1}{4}$ teaspoon baking soda + $\frac{1}{2}$ teaspoon cream of tartar

1 cup butter = 1 cup margarine

1 cup buttermilk = 1 tablespoon vinegar + regular milk to make 1 cup

1 cup buttermilk = $\frac{2}{3}$ cup plain yogurt + $\frac{1}{3}$ cup regular milk

1 ounce chocolate = 3 tablespoons cocoa + 1 tablespoon shortening

1 tablespoon cornstarch (for thickening) = 2 tablespoons flour

1 cup cream = $\frac{1}{2}$ cup butter + $\frac{3}{4}$ cup milk

1 small clove garlic = $\frac{1}{8}$ teaspoon garlic powder

1 tablespoon fresh herbs = 1 teaspoon dried herbs

1 cup honey = $1\frac{1}{4}$ cups sugar + $\frac{1}{4}$ cup water

1 cup fresh whole milk = 1 cup reconstituted dry milk + 2 teaspoons butter

1 cup fresh whole milk = $\frac{1}{2}$ cup evaporated milk + $\frac{1}{2}$ cup water

1 cup sour milk = 1 tablespoon lemon juice or vinegar + regular milk to make 1 cup

1 cup molasses = 1 cup honey

1 cup ricotta cheese = 1 cup cottage cheese + 1 tablespoon skim milk

1 cup sour cream = 1 cup yogurt

1 cup brown sugar = $\frac{3}{4}$ cup granulated sugar + $\frac{1}{4}$ cup molasses

$1\frac{1}{3}$ cups powdered sugar = 1 cup granulated sugar

1 cup yogurt = 1 cup buttermilk

All About Pasta and Noodles

For centuries, people all over the world have enjoyed eating pasta, whether in a processed form or as fresh dough. From Ramen noodles to linguini, all types of pasta are great to eat and inexpensive. Perfect for the cost-conscious college student like you!

What is it?

Macaroni is any pasta made from semolina flour and shaped in tubes. The most common kind is elbow macaroni, but there are dozens of other shapes. Spaghetti is pasta made in thin solid strings. Linguini is another spaghetti-like pasta that is flat and long. Noodles are pasta shaped in a ribbon form and are often made with eggs. Ramen noodles are very inexpensive and usually come with a flavor packet. All taste great!

Cooking Pasta

To cook any pasta, start with a saucepan at least half full of boiling water. Add the dry pasta (about 1 cup dry pasta to 4 cups of boiling water). When you first add the pasta, it will seem like there is too much water, but it will expand as it cooks. If you add too

Long spaghetti seems to defy being put in a pan of boiling water. Break it up if you want, but the long pieces will actually become limp and slide into the water. Just watch it carefully and stir it to keep from boiling over.

much pasta, it will soak up all the water and become sticky and gummy. Pasta only takes a few minutes to cook. Read the label of the container it came in—different shapes take different times to cook. Cook only until it is tender. Take a piece out of the water, let it cool a minute, and then bite into it. It should just be tender enough to bite through. Take the rest off the stove and drain. Eat right away. Rinse with cool water if you want to keep it from sticking.

About Poultry, Meat, and Eggs

First things first. Read the "sell by" or "use by" dates on everything you purchase. If you get something home and it doesn't look right or it smells funny, return it to the store as soon as possible. Otherwise throw it out. Use ground meats, fish, or poultry within a day or two of purchase, unless you freeze it for later use. If there's a bulge or dent in a can of tuna, it goes back, too. Look closely before putting items in your cart.

To coat chicken before you fry it, just drop it into a plastic bag filled with a little flour and seasonings.

Buying and Cooking Chicken or Turkey (Poultry)

- Choose poultry that looks and smells fresh. Chicken breasts come with the bone in or

Cook the chicken in a frying pan with a little oil until it is tender and no pink shows.

boneless, skin on or skinless. Boneless chicken breasts may cost a bit more, but they cook quickly and are versatile for many recipes.

- Keep poultry in the coldest part of the fridge, but not for more than 2 days. Defrost it in the refrigerator or microwave—never on the counter at room temperature. Rinse it off before cooking, and cook it until tender and until there is no sign of pink. Wash your hands after handling poultry.

Buying and Cooking Beef

- There are lots of beef cuts, from ground, steaks, roasts, and "other," which includes pot roast, brisket, and stew meat. Ask the butcher to help you.

- Know that "choice grade" cuts are more tender and more expensive than "select grade" cuts. Look for beef that is deep red and accented with white fat or marbling. Avoid packages where the meat has turned brown.

See the pink? Get rid of it! When browning ground beef, keep cooking it until the pink is all gone.

Now this is more like it! There isn't any pink left in this browned ground beef. It is ready to be used!

When you make beef patties, put a hole in the center of the raw meat. The heat will get to the middle faster and cook all the way through.

Pork: The Other White Meat

- Cuts of pork should be light pink and have a firm and lightly marbled (with fat) texture. Store in the coldest part of the fridge and use within 2 days of buying it. Cook it thoroughly as you do beef.

Deli Meats and Lunch Meats

- Purchase only what you think you will need for the next 3 or 4 days. Keep the meat refrigerated and wrapped tightly in plastic wrap. Opened packages should be used in 3 or 4 days. Unopened packages should keep until the "use by" date.

Buying Dairy Items and Eggs

- With milk, cottage cheese, sour cream, and yogurt, it is imperative that you check the "sell by" dates. Purchase the items with the farthest off dates. Check eggs, too. You don't want to buy cracked ones, which can be contaminated with bacteria. If you get up to the check-out counter and discover some of the eggs are cracked, just get a new dozen.

Cracking an Egg

- To crack an egg, just tap it on a cutting board or countertop and break it into a cup or bowl. Transfer it to the bowl you will be using for your recipe. That way you won't get shells in your finished food.

Cooking Eggs

- Eggs are a real bargain and there are so many ways to cook them. (However you cook them, be sure they are completely cooked. Don't eat raw or runny eggs.) You can scramble, poach, or fry them, make sandwiches with them, and use them in all kinds of recipes. Boiling is probably the easiest way to cook an egg and you can eat boiled eggs hot or cold.

Crack an egg on a cutting board or counter by gently tapping it. (Wash the surface after you do this!)

To boil an egg, place eggs (1 or more) in a single layer in a saucepan and add enough water to come at least 1 inch above the eggs. Cover, put on the burner on high, and

Move quickly to the cup and open the egg into the cup. Practice makes perfect.

quickly bring the water and eggs to just boiling. Boil 2 minutes. Turn off the heat and take them off the burner. Keep them covered and let them stand for about 10 minutes (for a large egg). Take off the lid and pour the hot water in the sink. Run cold water over the eggs until they are just cool enough to touch. Peel off the shell, put it on a plate, add some salt and pepper and enjoy! Refrigerate any leftover eggs in the shell and eat them cold later.

How to Buy and Prepare Fruits and Vegetables

Eat your fruits and veggies. No matter how hard you try, you should not live by pizza alone. There are great choices for fresh produce all year long. If you're smart—and we know you are—you'll take advantage of that fact.

Buying Fruits and Vegetables

- Produce sections of supermarkets have an abundance of fresh items. The frozen food cases are also good spots to choose vegetables and fruits. If you have a farmer's market in your area, this is a great way to get the freshest fruits and veggies that grow locally. Try some new ones!

- When you purchase salad greens, look for the darkest ones. Dark green translates to more nutrients. In fact, as a general rule, choose a rainbow of colors when you pick all your fruits and veggies—like orange carrots, red apples, green broccoli, blue blueberries—you get it now. You'll be more likely to get all the nutrients you need.

- Many kinds of salad makings come in bags. You don't have to clean, cut, chop, or even wash the pre-bagged greens if you don't want to. Just open the bag and close it when you're done. You do pay more for this convenience, of course.

To Prepare and Cook Vegetables

- Preparing veggies is a no-brainer. The easiest way for carrots, celery, broccoli, and others is to wash them and eat them fresh. Use a carrot peeler, if you like, to take off the outer skin of the carrots. Cut the ends off the celery and broccoli. Always wash the vegetables thoroughly. You don't need to use soap. Just use a lot of water.

This broccoli has been cooked too long. The texture is mushy and the broccoli has lost its pretty green color.

- Use a steamer. If you are lucky enough to have one, place the collapsible metal steamer over, (but not in) boiling water in a pan or covered pot. Depending on the density of the vegetable, it won't take long to steam them. Just a few minutes. Season as you wish.

This broccoli is just right to eat. It is tender but still a pretty green and has kept more of its nutrients.

- Use a pan. Start with about a cup of water and a dash of salt in a saucepan and bring it to a boil. Cut the vegetables into small pieces, drop them into the water, cover, and cook until just tender—for most veggies about 3 or 4 minutes. If you like crunchy vegetables, cook them a shorter amount of time.

- Use a microwave oven. Use a microwave-safe baking dish and add the veggies and a small amount of water. Cover and microwave. Remember, microwave oven powers differ, so times may differ, too.

- Use a wok or large skillet. To cook lots of veggies at once, make a stir-fry. Stir is the key word here. Simply heat about 3 tablespoons of vegetable oil in a wok or skillet. Add veggies and keep stirring until they are tender, but still a bit crisp. Add a little soy sauce if you wish, and cook and stir 2 minutes more. Serve as a vegetable dish or over rice.

To sauté vegetables such as onions, peppers, and celery (to add to soups or other dishes), cook until lightly browned in hot oil or butter.

- Sauté the veggies. Sautéing vegetables before using them in soups or casseroles brings out the flavor. Chop onions, celery, peppers, or whatever veggies you want to try into small pieces. Heat about 2 tablespoons of butter or oil in a saucepan on medium high and add the veggies. Cook until they are just browned—about 2 or 3 minutes. Even though it sounds pretty fancy, it is easy to do and these are great to use in soups and stews.

To slice and drain fruits and vegetables:

- Always cut citrus fruits (oranges, grapefruit, lemons, and limes) crosswise. This will make nicer slices and will be easier to squeeze the juice from the fruit.

To cut an orange or lemon to make slices or to squeeze out the juice, cut with the stem at the side.

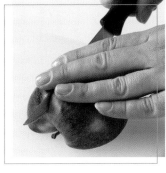

Cut apples or other crisp fruits or veggies with the knife blade down and your hand on top and out of the way.

- To squeeze the juice, use a juicer if you have one. If not, just cut the fruit in half and squeeze the juice from the fruit with your hands into a cup. Take out any of the seeds.

- When cutting apples or crisp fruit, be sure to cut with the blade facing down. Keep your hands away from the blade. Use a knife to take out the core after cutting the apple into fourths.

To drain chunky canned fruits, use a spoon to keep the fruit from draining out with the juice.

- To drain canned fruits and vegetables, open the can and then use a spoon or fork to keep the fruit or vegetable pieces from coming out with the juice. Don't use the can lid—it may cut you!

To drain canned vegetables, use a fork to keep the small veggies from draining out with the liquid.

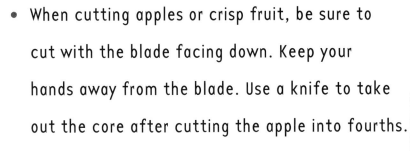

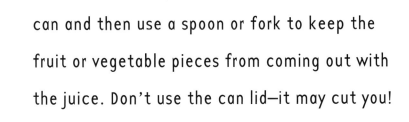

Baking

Baking is a way to provide yourself with a little comfort food during finals week or to impress your friends when you invite them over. The fabulous aromas you create when you make cookies or brownies will make you some new friends very quickly.

Some General Baking Hints

- Preheat your oven. In other words, if your cake is to bake at 350 degrees, let the oven warm up to that point before putting the pan full of batter into the oven. That way, it will bake more evenly and at the prescribed time.

- If the recipe calls for you to do it, grease your baking pan before pouring batter into it. Use no-stick cooking spray or a small amount of solid shortening. Just put the shortening in a little piece of waxed paper or paper towel and coat the bottom and sides of the pan evenly.

Put the solid shortening in a little piece of waxed paper or paper towel and coat the sides and bottom of the pan evenly.

- To help you in baking, you'll need these measuring tools: a set of measuring cups for dry ingredients, such as flour and sugar; measuring spoons; glass or plastic liquid measuring cup for oil, water, and other liquids; and a timer, if your stove doesn't have one.

- When you buy butter or margarine in the 1-pound boxes, it usually comes in quarters or sticks. The sticks are marked conveniently so you can cut off what you need. One stick of butter is equal to $1/2$ cup. Even the tablespoons are marked. How easy is that? If it isn't in sticks you'll have to measure it in a measuring cup or spoon, which is kind of messy. Don't use the margarine that comes in a tub. It doesn't work for baking.

This toothpick has unbaked batter on it. The cake isn't done. Put the cake back in the oven and check it again in a few minutes.

- When a recipe calls for brown sugar, it assumes that you measure it packed in the cup. Seems odd, but it is because the sugar is so moist and it is more consistently measured this way.

The toothpick came out clean and dry. The cake should be done. Take it out of the oven.

- To see if a baked item (such as a cake) is done, insert a toothpick near the center of the cake. If it comes out clean and dry, your item should be done. If it doesn't come out clean, bake the item a few more minutes and test again.

- To test doneness in custard-style puddings and pies like rice pudding or pumpkin pie, put the blade of a table knife into the middle of the pudding or pie. If the knife comes out clean with no runny batter or egg mixture clinging to the knife, the item should be done.

Weights and Measures

We're not all math majors, so here's a cheat sheet.

US Standard Equivalents

This is pretty basic, but stuff we all forget. So here's a little list for you to use.

3 teaspoons = 1 tablespoon

4 tablespoons = $^1/_4$ cup

$5^1/_3$ tablespoons = $^1/_3$ cup

8 tablespoons = $^1/_2$ cup

$10^2/_3$ tablespoons = $^2/_3$ cup

12 tablespoons = $^3/_4$ cup

16 tablespoons = 1 cup

1 cup = $^1/_2$ pint

2 cups = 1 pint

2 pints (4 cups) = 1 quart

4 quarts (16 cups) = 1 gallon

U.S./Standard Metric Equivalents

If you are a chemistry major, you might find these handy. The math doesn't come out perfectly when you switch back and forth, but here are the rounded versions.

$^1/_8$ teaspoon = .5 ml

$^1/_5$ teaspoon = 1 ml

$^1/_2$ teaspoon = 2.5 ml

1 teaspoon = 5 ml

1 tablespoon = 15 ml

2 tablespoons = 25 ml

1 fluid ounce = 30 ml

$^1/_3$ cup = 3 fluid ounces = 75 ml

$^1/_2$ cup = 4 fluid ounces =125 ml

$^2/_3$ cup = 5 fluid ounces = 150 ml

$^3/_4$ cup = 6 fluid ounces = 175 ml

1 cup = 8 fluid ounces = 250 ml

2 cups = 1 pint = 500 ml

1 quart = about 1 liter

Manners and Entertaining

This isn't about the usual weekend party. You know how to do that. This is about entertaining in a more formal way, or what to do if you're invited to a special affair. Maybe you'll be invited to a professor's home or be asked to host a party. It never hurts to know how to have a nice get-together or which spoon to use. Here are some entertaining ideas that might help you. After all, you will be famous some day.

A Nice Get-Together

- Bring out some candles and put soft music on the CD player. Yes, even though you are in college, it is okay to be a bit elegant once in a while. It will be fun. If you are invited to a special party or gathering, bring a small token of appreciation, like a plate of cookies or a box of candy.

- Depending on the situation, the number of guests, and the space available, you might want to set up for a buffet-style meal. That's an easy way to serve groups of 8 or more. Be logical. Put plates first, then the salad, main dish, vegetables, and bread. Put the dessert last. If a dish requires a sauce or condiment, put it right by the dish for easy serving.

- If guests won't be seated at a table, arrange silverware and napkins at the end of the line for easy pick-up. Have a separate table for drinks and possibly dessert, depending on your space.

Table Settings

There are many ways to set a table depending on what is served and how formal the event. Here are some ideas for how tables are set— you'll be glad you know how to do it and how to use it.

Very casual place setting

- Even if you use paper plates and canned soda, the knife (even if it is plastic) goes to the right of the plate and the fork and napkin at the left of the plate. Put the canned beverage or glass at the top right of the plate. When the party is over, put the cans in a sack. Don't stack them on the counter. (You never know when Mom or Dad may pay a surprise visit.)

Casual place setting

- Knife (blade edge in) and teaspoon are on the right of the dinner plate, with fork and napkin to the left. The glass is above the knife. If soup is to be served, the soup spoon goes to the right of the teaspoon and if salad is served, a salad fork is placed to the left of dinner fork. Cup and saucer or mug are at the right.

Informal place setting

- Knife (blade edge in) and teaspoon go to the right of the dinner plate, with dinner fork and salad fork to the left in order of use. Goblet and wine glass go to upper right above knife and spoon. Bread plate with butter knife goes above two forks on left.

Formal sit-down dinners

- To the right of the plate is the knife (blade edge in) and then teaspoon. The soup spoon and dessert fork are at the top of the plate. The forks are placed to the left of the plate in order of use from outside in, salad and dinner forks. Glasses are above the knife. Left to right, water goblet, then wine glasses, placed large to small. The bread plate, with bread knife across it, goes above the forks. Salad plate goes to the left of the forks (not shown), and cup and saucer (sometimes with coffee spoon) go to the right of the setting. Usually, however, those are brought to the table when served.

Nutrition

"You are what you eat." You've heard it before, and for good reason—it's true. Think about it—what you put in your body will determine how well you think and how healthy you are. That is why every box, can, and jar has to put the nutritional facts on it. Look at the examples of the nutritional labels shown on the opposite page and you'll learn how to read them.

- It is important to remember that all the percentages on Nutrition Fact Labels are based on a 2000-calorie per day diet, but depending on your gender and size, this may not be the correct number of calories for you to consume. Depending on physical activity level, women should consume 1500–2500 calories per day, and men should consume 2000–3000 calories per day.

- Try to have a fairly consistent eating schedule, eating your meals at about the same time every day. This will keep your digestive system in the best shape.

- Drink 8 glasses of water per day to stay hydrated, decrease hunger, and keep your skin and cells healthy and strong.

- Eating a piece of fruit before your meal, such as an apple or orange, will assure you of more vitamins and minerals and will probably leave you less hungry for junk food. Give it a try.

- Focus on eating lots of fruits, vegetables, whole grains, and low-fat dairy products. These are all high in vitamins and minerals, low in fat, sodium, and calories, and are delicious! Eat up!

Nutrition Facts
Serving Size 2 Tbsp (32g)
Servings Per Container about 15

Amount Per Serving

Calories 190   Calories from Fat 140

	% Daily Value*
Total Fat 17g	26%
Saturated Fat 3.5g	18%
Cholesterol 0mg	0%
Sodium 150mg	6%
Total Carbohydrate 7g	2%
Dietary Fiber 2g	8%
Sugars 3g	
Protein 7g	

Vitamin A 0%	•	Vitamin C 0%	
Calcium 0%	•	Iron 2%	
Niacin 20%	•	Vitamin E 10%	

* Percent Daily Values are based on a 2,000 calorie diet.

This section tells you the types and amount of carbohydrates in the food. Generally you want the most fiber and least sugar possible.

This section tells you the vitamins and minerals in the food item. Your goal is to have 100% of all the vitamins and minerals every day.

This section shows you all the ingredients in the food and also any important allergy information.

Always look at the serving size, which tells you the reference size being used to determine the nutrition facts.

This section shows you the types and amounts of fat in the food. You always want the least saturated fat and trans fat possible.

These are the recommended intakes for an average person with a 2000-calorie per day diet.

Nutrition Facts
Serving Size 1/2 cup (56g)
Servings Per Container 8

Amount Per Serving	Cereal	Cereal with 1/2 cup Vit. A & D Fat Free Milk
Calories	240	280
Calories from Fat	50	50

	% Daily Value**	
Total Fat 6g*	9%	9%
Saturated Fat 1g	5%	5%
Trans Fat 0g		
Cholesterol 0mg	0%	0%
Sodium 130mg	5%	8%
Potassium 170mg	5%	10%
Total Carb. 40g	13%	15%
Dietary Fiber 4g	16%	16%
Sugars 13g		
Protein 6g		

Vitamin A	0%	4%
Vitamin C	0%	0%
Calcium	2%	15%
Iron	12%	12%
Vitamin D	2%	15%

*Amount in cereal. One half cup fat free milk contributes an additional 40 calories, 65mg sodium, 6g total carbohydrates (6g sugars) and 4g protein.

**Percent Daily Values are based on a 2,000 calorie diet. Your daily values may be higher or lower depending on your calorie needs.

		Calories	2,000	2,500
Total Fat	Less than		65g	80g
Sat. Fat	Less than		20g	25g
Cholesterol	Less than		300mg	300mg
Sodium	Less than		2,400mg	2,400mg
Total Carbohydrate			300g	375g
Dietary Fiber			25g	30g

INGREDIENTS: ROLLED OATS, EVAPORATED CANE JUICE, EXPELLER PRESSED CANOLA OIL, DEFATTED WHEAT GERM, OAT FLOUR, BROWN RICE SYRUP, MOLASSES, SALT, NATURAL FLAVOR, SOY LECITHIN.

ALLERGY INFORMATION: MANUFACTURED ON EQUIPMENT THAT PROCESSES PRODUCTS CONTAINING PEANUTS AND OTHER NUTS.

Buying Groceries

Okay, here's something to ponder. When you go to the supermarket, notice that the healthiest foods for you to buy are around the perimeter of the store. If you could only shop the outer rim, you'd be choosing fresh fruits and vegetables, meat, and milk and dairy products. It's when you go down the center aisles that you encounter packaged and processed foods, candies, soda pop, and snack foods.

From the foods on the end aisles to those at the checkout counter, products are purposely placed there to entice you and encourage impulse buying. That's why when you meant to get only a gallon of milk, you came home with three bags of groceries.

Some Shopping Points to Ponder:

- Buy produce during the week, since most deliveries come in on weekdays. The produce will be fresher!

- Try to stay within your budget. Shop when you aren't hungry.

- The ends of the aisles often display something new or something in season. Don't be tempted if it's not something you want or need.

- Stay focused on your purchases by making a list and sticking to it. If your roommate asks you to buy something for him or her, be sure to keep a list to track what is what or you may not get paid back. Oh well, you probably owe your friend money anyway.

- Check expiration or "sell by" dates on all products. Buy the ones with the farthest off date, of course.

- The express lane at the grocery store isn't always shorter. Studies have shown that the wait is almost identical, because more transactions take place. Go with what seems to be the shortest line, express or not.

- Supermarket shelves are planned to attract your eye. At the top are smaller, regional, and gourmet brands. These smaller brands don't have the budgets to pay for better placement. The "bull's-eye zone," or eye level, is the best placement.

- Colleges get a lot of free coupons to pass out and some are really a bargain. Others are for things you would never use. Sometimes they are a great incentive to try something new—sometimes they are for things you just don't need. You decide.

- You can buy groceries at farmer's markets and may save money because the produce is seasonal and very available.

- To avoid crowds, many experts advise shopping on Tuesday, the least busy day of the week.

- Paper or plastic? Whatever you choose, recycle them.

Clean Up Your Act

Really, it's true. You'll feel more efficient and productive if your surroundings don't look like a pig pen. Where to begin?

- Everything has its place. Easier said than done, but the plan does work.

- The countertop, the table, your desk. All are good places to put things. Clean 'em up. Research shows you'll feel much, much better. In the kitchen, you'll cut down on bacteria that can cause food poisoning. Wash the dishes at least every couple days—every day is best. It only takes a few minutes—just do it!

- Respect fire and what it can do. Never cook over an open flame with long hair in your face. Don't cook in long, flowing sleeves. If something happens, stop, drop and roll.

- If you have a grease fire, throw the contents of a box of baking soda on the fire. Always have a box handy. Don't throw water on it! That will spread a grease fire. Make sure you have a smoke detector (that works!) and a fire extinguisher and that you know where it is.

- Clean up as you go along. It makes the task less daunting at the end.

- While you talk on your cell phone, pick up around your house or unload the dishwasher at the same time. It could liven up a boring conversation if nothing else.

- Declutter, sort, and store or toss before you start cleaning.

- On a daily basis, spray and wipe down counters, sweep the floor, and scrub the kitchen sink.

- Add lemon juice to your dishwater to make dishes sparkle.

- Have wood floors? Have pets? Get an enzymatic cleaner at a pet store. Don't allow liquid to pool on the floors.

- Clean your carpet every 12 to 18 months and vacuum frequently.

- To rid the microwave of unpleasant odors, wipe the interior with a solution of 4 tablespoons baking soda to 1 quart warm water. Do not use commercial oven cleaner in a microwave.

- To get rid of smells in the kitchen sink drain, dump half a box of baking soda and wait a few minutes before running water. (Notice the baking soda trend? It is good stuff and cheap!)

- Never pour fat down the drain. It will probably clog it. Plumber bills are no fun.

- To rid a cutting board of the odor of chopped onion or garlic, scrub it with baking soda.

- If you spill wine or juice, spritz the area with club soda, blot, and repeat until the stain is gone. Use white vinegar to remove soft drink stains. It really works.

What To Do When You're Sick

There is nothing worse than being sick—especially when you are away from home. And Mom or Dad would love to be there to make you chicken soup and gelatin. But if you can't go home, and if Mom and Dad aren't near, here are some tips to get you through this and to make it a little better—even if you are alone.

- Make sure you know where the campus student health service is located. Call them if you need help. They can check for colds, flu, and sore throats and provide X-rays, psychiatric screenings, allergy shots, and lab services.

- If you live alone, be sure that someone knows you aren't well. Have them check in with you.

- Communicate with your professors. They are more understanding if they know what's going on.

- Plan in advance what you should do in case of illness and you're a long way from home. Is there a family friend nearby to help?

- Reinforce healthy habits, because a healthy immune system can fight off infection more easily.

- Confidentiality is not a problem. In fact, it's the law.

- If you are seriously ill, don't be shy. Call 911.

- What to eat when you are sick? Well, that depends on what you have. Most doctors and nurses often have the same response: If you have had the stomach flu with vomiting and diarrhea, (oh yeah, the fun stuff), after your stomach settles down, start with clear liquids such as chicken broth or the broth from chicken noodle soup—just a teaspoon at first. Try gelatin such as Jell-O and lemon-lime soda, too. If that stays down, try dry white toast and a boiled egg. Don't have any dairy for a couple of days. Take it slow. Your system has been angry, so make up to it nicely. If you have a cold or upper respiratory infection, chicken noodle soup is good to open up the sinuses. Really, any kind of soup is good to make your throat feel better. A little honey in some hot tea will help, too. When in doubt, call someone who knows. Everyone needs a little tender loving care once in awhile. They'll be glad to help you.

Phone Numbers:

Emergency Room: _ _ _ _ _ _ _ _ _ _

Doctor: _ _ _ _ _ _ _ _ _ _ _ _ _ _

Home: _ _ _ _ _ _ _ _ _ _ _ _ _ _

Mom cell: _ _ _ _ _ _ _ _ _ _ _ _

Dad cell: _ _ _ _ _ _ _ _ _ _ _ _

Poison Control: _ _ _ _ _ _ _ _ _

Roommate Cell: _ _ _ _ _ _ _ _ _

Best Friend Cell: _ _ _ _ _ _ _ _

Boyfriend or _ _ _ _ _ _ _ _ _ _

Girlfriend Cell: _ _ _ _ _ _ _ _
(use pencil)

Make It This Size

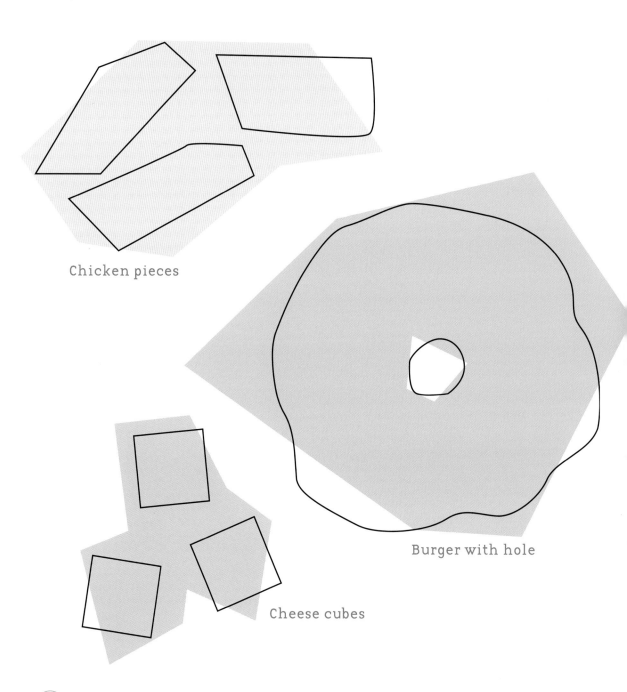

Chicken pieces

Burger with hole

Cheese cubes

Here's a handy real-life guide to how big to make some of the food items in this book. You don't have to make them exactly like this, of course, but it might give you an idea of about how big they usually are—so you don't have a cookie the size of a plate or a hamburger the size of a golf ball. Whatever.

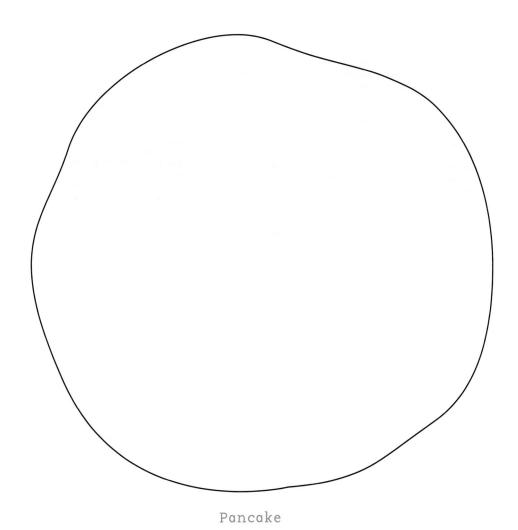

Pancake

Make it this size

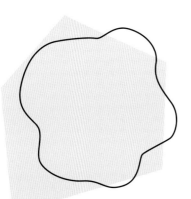

Chocolate
Oatmeal Drop
Cookie

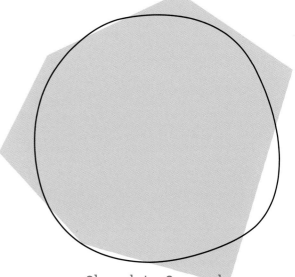

Chocolate-Covered
Crispy Ball

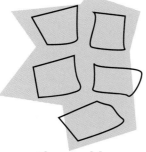

Chopped ham
pieces

Chocolate Chunk
Cookie (before it
is baked)

Fruit Pizza crust

Glossary

Foods that need a little explanation

Cardamom: A spice with a warm, sweet-spicy flavor popular in Scandinavia and India.

Chicken Broth: Liquid and flavors left over when you cook a chicken. You can buy it in a can with the canned soup. Common brands are Swanson or Campbell's.

Cocoa Powder: A powder form of chocolate used in cooking. Often used to make hot chocolate.

Corn Syrup: A very thick, sugary white syrup—you buy it in a big bottle usually. A common brand is Karo Syrup.

Cream Cheese: A white soft cheese that comes in a tub or wrapped in foil. Often used on bagels or in cooking.

Cup-of-Soup Mix: Dry packets of soup mix you buy, such as Lipton brand.

Ground Beef: Hamburger

Lean Hamburger: Hamburger with a low percentage of fat, like 10% fat or lower.

No-Stick Cooking Spray: Essentially grease in a can—a very handy thing. A common brand is Pam.

Non-Fat Dry Milk: Milk that comes powder form. Add water to make milk.

Non-Dairy Creamer: A substance used as a substitute for cream. Comes in dry packets or jars.

Oatmeal: Another name is rolled oats. It can be bought in two ways: old-fashioned or quick-cooking. Old-fashioned is bigger, whole pieces of oats, and quick-cooking is smaller, broken-up pieces of oats. A common brand is Quaker Oats.

Picante Sauce: A spicy chile sauce used on Mexican food similar to salsa.

Pizza Sauce: Thick tomato sauce with some other added spices and stuff made especially for pizza-making. You can buy it in a can near the other tomato sauce products.

Poultry: Chicken, turkey, goose, or other domestic birds.

Powdered Sugar: Sugar ground up very, very fine so it is powdered; you can buy it in bags, and it may also be called confectioner's sugar.

Processed Cheese: Cheese that has been specially made to melt easily, such as the brand Velveeta.

Rice: A common grain. Comes as raw or real rice in brown or white. Also comes as instant rice that cooks quickly.

Cooking terms that are used a lot

Bake: Cook food in an oven (like cookies, cakes, etc.).

Beat: To mix ingredients together until they are smooth. This is more than just mixing. It means to mix it rapidly with with spoon or fork or even an electric mixer if you have one.

Boil: Cook food in a liquid over high heat. When boiling you will see many large bubbles that rapidly rise from the bottom of the pan and pop at the water's surface.

Broil: Cook food by using the direct heat of the broiler at the top of the oven.

Brown: Cook food, usually in a frying pan, until it looks brown.

Chill: Put food in the refrigerator to make it cold.

Chop: To cut up into little pieces about the same size.

Combine: Mix it together.

Cool: Let food stand out on the counter (or wire rack) until it is not hot.

Drain: Take the liquid from the product. You can do this lots of ways. One way is to put the food in a sieve or strainer to separate the liquid part from the solid part.

Fry: Cook food in a frying pan with grease.

Grate: Rub the food over the smallest holes on the grater to make little pieces.

Grease: Put some sort of fat onto a surface to prevent food from sticking to the surface (like using no-stick spray coating or a piece of butter or margarine).

Melt: Making something solid (like butter) into liquid (like melted butter) by heating it in the microwave or on the stove.

Microwave-Safe: Anything that is safe to put in the microwave. It is important to check to see if the bowl or whatever you are using is microwave-safe (read the bottom of the bowl) or it might melt or break.

Mix: Stir ingredients together so the mixture looks the same everywhere.

Peel: Remove the outer skin from fruits or vegetables, using your hands or a peeler.

Rolling Boil: When boiling, this is a rapid boil, which will cook foods quickly.

Salt and Pepper to Taste: Add enough spice to please you.

Sauté: To add ingredients to hot oil or grease to brown it. This is usually done to vegetables or small pieces of meat.

Shred: Rub the food over a larger hole on a grater to make long, thin pieces.

Slice: To cut something into into thin pieces that are about the same size.

Sift: You probably will never do this, but it means to put flour or other powdered baking item in a sifter to remove any lumps and to make it all fine and nice.

Simmer: After food has boiled, cook food on top of the stove over low heat, seeing small bubbles for a long time.

Stir-fry: To cook something quickly in a little bit of hot oil on top of the stove.

Mom's Recipes

Mom's Recipes

101 Answers

Eggs *page 25*
1. If you can unscramble this one, you can get your Ph.D. right now.
2. A. True
3. C. Carl Fabergé, the court jeweler for the Czar of Russia, did those.
4. C. Delmonico's, the first restaurant or public dining room in the United States, created for Mrs. LeGrand Benedict.

Rice *page 35*
1. False. Wild Rice is actually the seeds of a grass.
2. B.
3. True—you can eat lots!
4. A. Yup, a long time ago.

Bagels *page 37*
1. C. Isn't that weird?
2. A. Pregnant Women. Whatever.
3. B. That is without the cream cheese, of course.

Oatmeal *page 39*
1. Pick one, any one.
2. B. He is not an actual person, but his image is that of a man dressed in Quaker garb. He projects honesty, strength, and wholesomeness.
3. C. That would be 1966.
4. C. Ah, cookies.

Spiced Applesauce *page 51*
1. A. It goes with everything, but especially pork.
2. C. It has been "on the side" since Medieval times.
3. B. Moses knew his cinnamon.
4. A., B., and C—everyone paid big bucks

Hot Dogs *page 57*
1. C. Would you believe 150 million doggies?
2. C.
3. B. He is so cute.

Pita Bread *page 59*
1. A. Round
2. B.
3. It's baked at high temperatures, causing the rounds of dough to puff up. Once out of the oven, pita flattens, but the baked dough remains separated inside. It's magic!
4. A., B., and C. They are good with most anything.

Chili *page 65*
1. A. Where else? Texas has been known for its Chili worldwide!
2. B. Beans are taboo!
3. A.
4. C. Ya-hoo!

Chocolate *page 77*
1. A. Christopher Columbus, that lucky dog. Man, that guy discovered everything worthwhile.
2. C. A nice big fat turkey.
3. B. Plain chocolate is very, very bitter—you can taste this if you eat pure dark chocolate. The sweet chocolate we are used to gets it sweetness from lots of added sugar, and sometimes vanilla and cinnamon as well.
4. C. Thomas Jefferson. No wonder the Declaration of Independence is so brilliant.

Carrots *page 78*
1. B. Usually
2. A. Give the credit to the Dutch growers who bred the vegetable to grow in the colors of the House of Orange.
3. A. True
4. B. No. The baby carrots have about 70 percent as much beta carotene – the good stuff. However, you're likely to eat more of the baby carrots.

Peanut Butter *page 89*
1. A., B., and C. As early as the 15th century, Africans ground up peanuts. The Chinese were known to crush peanuts into sauces. Soldiers in the Civil War made peanut porridge.
2. C. Before they got into cereals, Dr. John Kellogg and his brother W.K. tried to develop a vegetarian source of protein. C.H. Sumner introduced peanut butter at the St. Louis World's Fair in 1904.
3. C. George Washington Carver, of course.
4. B. Elvis, the King.

Apples *page 106*
1. A. So true.
2. B. 80 calories—you can eat two.
3. A. Apples are actually a member of the rose family.
4. A. Michigan

Yogurt *page 121*
1. All three, of course, but this is a cookbook. So C. Yogurt is a fermented culture.
2. B. That would be milk.
3. B. Genghis Khan had a yogurt mustache.
4. All three—eat up!

Popcorn *page 132*
1. A. Mexico—a long time ago
2. A. It appears to be true.
3. A and B—Nebraska and Indiana.
4. C. Watching TV, because attendance at movie theaters dropped.

Coffee *page 141*
1. B. Coffee, with almost 2 billion cups drunk every day worldwide.
2. A. The American Revolution.
3. C. Turkey – all the way. Turkish law makes it legal for a woman to divorce her husband if he fails to provide her with her daily quota of coffee.
4. C. The heavy tax on tea imposed in 1773 was a sign of the colonists dependence on Britain, so many Americans switched to drinking coffee instead. To drink coffee was an expression of freedom.

SOURCES:
Popcorn.org
Hungrymonster.com
Peanutbutterlovers.com
Canadaegg.ca
Whatscookingamerica.net
Hot-dog.org
Iowa Beef Industry
Quakeroatmeal.com
Wikipedia.com
Historyforkids.org
University of Illinois Extension

Index

A-B

Apples 107
Applesauce 50
Bagels 36
Baked Apples 107
Baking 160-161
Bananas 21, 120
Basic Food Supplies 16-17
Beanie Weenies 56
Beans 56
Biscuits 91
Breadsticks 128
Broccoli 26, 157
Brownies 88
Burgers 60
Buying groceries 40-41, 168-169

C

Cabbage 109
Cabbage Salad 108
Cake 96, 100
Caramel Corn 133
Carrots 79, 118
Carrot Casserole 118
Casseroles 62, 98, 118
Cheese 29, 44, 46, 52, 58, 60, 64, 70, 98, 114, 118, 126, 138
Cherry Chocolate Cupcakes 96
Cherry Pie Filling 96
Chicken 48, 54, 152-153
Chicken and Rice 54
Chicken Veggie Soup 22
Chili 64
Chocolate 82, 88, 96, 134, 136

Chocolate Chunk Cookies 134
Chocolate-Covered Crispy Balls 136
Chocolate Oatmeal Drops 83
Cleaning Up 170-171
Cocoa 76
Coconut 83, 112
Coffee 140
Cookies 83, 134, 136
Cooking Equipment 12-15
Corn 95
Corn bread 95
Cream Cheese 79
Cupcakes 96

D-F

Double Chicken Noodle Soup 92
Draining Vegetables and Fruit 159
Egg Casserole 98
Eggs 24, 32, 98, 152, 154-155
Egg Sandwich 24
Entertaining 142-143, 163-165
Food Safety 146-149
Food Substitutions 150
French Toast 32
Fruit 112, 116, 120, 130, 156, 159
Fruit and Veggie Facts 122-123
Fruit Pizza 116-117

G-L

Glossary 178-181
Good Ol' Chile 64
Granola 72
Ground Beef 44, 52, 60, 64, 126, 138, 153
Ham 58, 98
Hot Cocoa 76
Hot Dog Bagel 36
Hot Dogs 56

Hot Spiced Applesauce 50
Labels 149
Lasagna 126
Lemon Cake 100

M-O

Macaroni 46
Mac n' Cheese 46
Marshmallows 76, 136
Meat 152-154
Mexican Salad Crisps 110
Milk 76
Noodles 62, 92, 120, 126, 151
Nutrition 166-167
Nutrition Labels 167
Oatmeal 72, 80, 83
Oranges 108

P

Pancakes 21
Parfait 130
Pasta 44, 46, 62, 151
Peanut Butter 21, 74, 88
Peanut Butter and Banana Pancakes 21
Peanut Butter Brownies 88
Peanuts 133
Peas 46, 62, 92
Pita Treat 58
Pizza Boats 52
Popcorn 132
Pork 154
Potato 26
Poultry 152-153
Power Bars 80
Pudding 34
Quesadillas 114

R-S

Raisins 34, 50, 72, 79, 80
Ramen Noodles 48, 108
Rice 54
Rice Pudding 34
Salad Crisps 110
Sandwiches 24, 29, 74, 79
Sesame Seed Breadsticks 128
Soups 22, 92
Spaghetti 44
Spiced Coffee 140
Strawberries 113, 116
Stir-Fry 48
Stuffed Potato 26
Sweet Fruit Salad 112
Sweet Peanut Butter Sandwiches 74

T-Z

Taco Cheese Dip 138
Take-Along Tips 84-85
Tomatoes 44, 64
Tortillas 110, 114
Tortilla Chips 138
Tuna 9
Tuna Melt 19
Tuna Casserole 62
Using Packaged Items 102-103
Vegetable Soup 22
Vegetables 26, 48, 156-158
Yogurt 120, 130
Yogurt Smoothie 120
Weights and Measures 162
When You're Sick 172-173
Wraps 70

About the Author:

Carol Field Dahlstrom

has produced over 75 crafts, food, decorating, children's, and holiday books for Better Homes and Gardens®, Bookspan®, and from her own publishing company, Brave Ink Press. She has made numerous television, radio, and speaking appearances sharing her books and demonstrating simple ways to make life happier and more fulfilling. Her creative vision and experience make her books fun as well as informative. She is actually a great cook with two children in college—one that can cook—the other needs this book.

Acknowledgements:

Lyne Neymeyer (book designer) has designed dozens of books for various leading publishers across the country. She also teaches book design at the university level and brings her fresh and creative approach to every book she creates. A photographer as well as a designer, Lyne's talents are many—although she really can't cook at all. She has vowed to use this book so she won't have to eat old Pop Tarts.

Andy Lyons (photographer) is best known for his unique and creative approach to photographing people. Based in Des Moines, Iowa, Andy is also a well-known and talented food, crafts, and decorating photographer. His work can be seen in major books and magazines across the country. He is a great cook but uses way too much garlic.

Dean Tanner (photographer) is a multi-talented photographer. His beautiful food photography can be seen in Cuisine® magazine as well as other publications. You can also see many of his well-known photos on vegetable and fruit cans across the world. As well as a great photographer, he is a fine cook and loves to eat all the food after a photo shoot.

Nancy Degner (consultant) As Executive Director for the Iowa Beef Industry Council, Nancy is responsible for overseeing all promotion, education, and research programs. Nancy has degrees in Food and Nutrition/ Food Science and Home Economics Education and is a member of the Iowa State Food Safety Task Force. She is a talented and awesome cook and is always making new and interesting recipes for her friends and family—usually with beef.

Janet Figg (consultant) An editor and food guru for more than 25 years, Janet has edited dozens of food magazines for Better Homes and Gardens® Special Interest Publications. Considered an expert in everything about food and the kitchen, her very favorite thing is cookies—both making them and eating them.

Jennifer Peterson (consultant) A well-known food stylist and food artist, Jennifer graduated with a degree in Food and Nutrition and began her career in the Better Homes and Gardens® Test Kitchen. She has also worked extensively with the food magazine, Cuisine®, as a consultant and food stylist. She and her husband now have three darling children and she cooks amazing meals for them all.

Special thanks to our college-kid models—
Robin, Michael, Lizzy, Adrian, Adam, Marcia, Allison, and Bonnie. We know you'll all be great cooks someday.

Allison May (art illustrator) is a senior in college majoring in graphic design. As a young and talented artist, she brings a playful style and cleverness to her illustrations, making them a delight to look at. She can cook a little bit, but prefers candy and ice cream.

Elizabeth Dahlstrom (writer) is a senior in college majoring in Nutrition. She knows what is healthy to eat and shares that with her friends when they eat junk. She is always trying weird recipes with ingredients you can't find anywhere. She is actually a really good cook and loves to make strange overly-nutritious breads.

Other Books from Brave Ink Press

If you like this book, look for other
books from Carol Field Dahlstrom Inc.
and Brave Ink Press

- **Simply Christmas**
- **Christmas—Make it Sparkle**
- **Beautiful Christmas**
- **An Ornament a Day**

And from the Creative Bone Series:

- **Cool Crafts to Make—even if you don't
  have a Creative Bone in your body!**

To order books
e-mail us at braveink@aol.com or
visit us at www.braveink.com

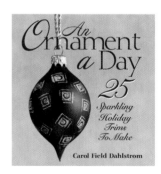

Brave Ink Press—the "I can do that!" books